Translation Talks

Translation Talks

통번역입문

Jang, Minho

한국문화사

Translation Talks
통번역입문

초판인쇄 2012년 2월 25일
초판발행 2012년 2월 28일

지 은 이 장 민 호
꾸 민 이 이 지 은
펴 낸 이 김 진 수
펴 낸 곳 **한국문화사**
등   록 1991년 11월 9일 제2-1276호
주   소 서울특별시 성동구 아차산로 3(성수동 1가) 502호
전   화 (02)464-7708 / 3409-4488
전   송 (02)499-0846
이 메 일 hkm7708@hanmail.net
홈페이지 www.hankookmunhwasa.co.kr

책값은 뒤표지에 있습니다.

잘못된 책은 바꾸어 드립니다.

ISBN 978-89-5726-951-0   93740

■ Preface: To the Student

Translation is not just a language learning process. The first reason to practice translation is that it will help you communicate more clearly and concisely in a more reader-friendly way. Translation is a form of communication involving more than one language. Successful translation requires world knowledge, proficiency in both source and target languages and knowhow of delivering the message in an economic and efficient way. Consequently, the characteristics required of good translators are also some of the essential traits required in a good leader. The second reason to practice translation is that it will help you have a broad knowledge of the world you live in. Translators first have to be interested in the topic of the text they work on. Taking interest in something often means knowing better about it than about other topics. As translation students you may have to cope with the text of a topic in which you may not be much interested in. From my experience as a translation teacher, many students, especially female ones, feel uncomfortable dealing with text about such 'hard' issues as those full of military and political contents. Economic and IT related topics are not much less tough for them, either. Successful translators would be better off by having at least a little knowledge on as many topics as possible. This superficial but broad-ranging knowledge has a synergistic effect to help the translator understand more easily new topics he has never dealt with before. The third reason to practice translation is that it will help you summarize what other people tell and write. Visualization simplifies the message in the source text so that you can depict the visual image with words you choose, in an order you choose, and more importantly, at a length you choose. Once the translator has visualized the text, it is not the words that matter, but the overall message of the original. To visualize the message, you have to read the entire source text before proceeding. Time spent in the visualization process will be compensated tenfold later and will prove to be time-saving for the entire task. A good leader has to have a more balanced view on things happening both at home and abroad. And based on that view, she must develop a future vision on when, how and where to take her organization- to lead and help it prosper. A good translator takes advantage of her ability to translate by becoming the first to know what is happening in the world, and becoming the first to interpret and deliver it to the members of her organization. Students must understand that translation is a trait, not simply a skill to earn a living as a profession. I hope that this book will help them understand the true nature of translation and gain an insight into translation, one of the longest-lasting practices and professions of mankind.

Minho Jang
February, 2012

■ 서문

통번역은 요약과 창작 능력, 배경 지식, 두 개 언어에 대한 구사 능력, 그리고 문화적 이해 등이 복합적으로 요구되는 고도의 지적 활동이다. 이 책은 대학에서 처음으로 통번역 관련 과목을 수강하는 학습자들을 위한 입문서이다.

각 장의 도입 부분에서는 통번역이라는 지적 활동이 갖는 의미를 각기 다른 관점에서 설명함으로써 수강자들이 통번역 이론이나 학설에 대한 사전 지식 없이도 통번역의 본질을 보다 직관적으로 이해할 수 있도록 하였다. 이어서 번역 텍스트(Text for Today)를 제시하여 도입 부분에서 얻은 직관적인 이해를 바탕으로 수강자들이 나름대로 통번역을 실습할 수 있도록 하였다. 이 과정에서 교수가 개입함으로써 교육의 효과를 극대화할 수 있을 것이다. 또한 대다수 통번역 입문 과정 수강자들이 영어의 학습자이기도 한 점을 고려하여 번역 텍스트 중 유용하게 쓰일 수 있는 구문을 찾아 정리, 제시하였다. 이는 학습자들이 영어 텍스트를 읽으면서 유용하다고 생각되는 표현을 스스로 찾아 정리하는 습관을 갖게 하며 자연스러운 번역문을 생산하는데 기여한다.

이어 회화 연습(Talking Practice)에서는 번역 텍스트에서 다룬 주제로 프리 토킹을 할 수 있도록 대화를 예시(Model Dialogue)하였다. 이는 또한 동일한 주제의 통역을 실습하기 위한 예비 단계이다.

리뷰 테스트(Review Test)에서는 빈 칸 채우기를 통해 수강자들이 번역 텍스트를 얼마나 잘 이해하고 있는지를 점검한다. 빈 칸 채우기는 단순한 암기력을 체크하는 것이 아니라 해당 문장의 번역을 위해 수강자가 얼마나 고민하였는가를 간접적으로 체크한다. 테스트의 후반부는 반대 방향으로의 번역(back translation)을 통해 수강자가 모국어의 간섭에서 벗어나 정확하게 영어 원문으로 되돌아 갈 수 있는지를 체크한다. 이는 자연스러운 번역을 위한 연습이자 동시에 영작문에서 콩글리쉬를 방지하는 연습이기도 하다.

번역의 다양한 주제에 관한 텍스트를 번역하다 보면 단순히 읽고 이해하는 것보다 텍스트의 의미를 보다 깊이 음미하게 될 것이다.

이 책은 모두 10개의 장으로 구성되어 있다. 이는 대학에서 한 한기의 수업이 통상 12~14회 정도이지만 한 개의 장을 한 번의 수업에서 모두 소화하기 어렵다는 점을 감안한 것이다. 원활한 수업 진도를 위해 정규 수업에서는 도입 부문 강독(또는 번역), 번역 텍스트 일부에 대한 번역 실습, 그리고 회화 연습을 다루고 나머지는 수강자의 자율 학습에 맡겨도 될 것이다.

■ Table of Contents

Chapter 1 — Translation as Reading the World We Live in

Intellectual Curiosity

Translators first have to be interested in the topic of the text they work on. Taking interest in something often means knowing better about it than about other topics. As translation students you may have to cope with the text of a topic in which you are not much interested in. From my experience as a translation teacher, many students, especially female ones, feel uncomfortable dealing with text about such 'hard' issues as those full of military and political connotations. Economic and IT related topics are not much less tough for them either. Successful translators, as the title of this chapter implies, would be better off by having at least a little knowledge on as many topics as possible. This superficial but broad-ranging knowledge has a synergistic effect to help the translator understand more easily new topics he has never dealt with before.

Translation topics are usually not that easy. If they were easy enough, the job of translating them would not have reached you as a professional translator in the first place. But it does not necessarily mean that you have to be curious about everything in this world. You can't do that and, more importantly, you don't have to do that. The world knowledge, or background knowledge for translation, can be divided into four categories: politics, economy, society, and culture. As the society we live in gets more complex and diversified, the four categories do not seem to include all phenomena taking place on earth. But no matter how complex and diversified the society gets, almost everything can fall under one of the four pieces of 'world knowledge.'

Among the four divisions of knowledge, economy seems to be the most important these days. In modern times, knowledge is treated and traded as economic goods. That is why most graduate schools of translation and interpretation have 'economic principles' course in their curricula. World affairs, seemingly military and diplomatic, have their roots in economic motives. For example, America's military operations in Iraq, some argue, had their ulterior motives in economics. More recently, the civil unrest and its resulting subversion of the Mubarak government, seemingly a pure political affair, was also triggered by some economic situations.

The beauty of being a student translator or a pro translator is to appreciate, interpret, and if necessary, create the message the author tries to convey. In this respect, the translator has as much, or sometimes more leeway than the author. The debate whether or not translators could create the originally intended meaning by the author has been around for a very long time, maybe since the practice of translating began. But in real life, a combination of translation and creation is better received in the market than a faithfully, word-for-word translated version. That's especially true in the subtitling market. In this specific market, who the subtitler is often decides how much the box office revenue will be. So, translating is often a highly market-oriented activity. Translating is, therefore, a very purpose-oriented and reader-oriented activity.

When it comes to translating, having knowledge not only means knowledge about an affair or object, but also means knowledge on the vocabulary and on how to express it naturally and concisely in the target language. A typical translation teacher, therefore, requests his students to create a long glossary before working on the translation task.

Students who lack the relevant background knowledge on the topic in question tend to translate, word for word, and thus end up producing a much longer version than the original. Let's take 9.11 for example. Suppose you now are working on a text about 9.11. As you may easily understand, the three digits means '*the infamous terrorist attack on the World Trade Center Buildings in Manhattan, New York on September 11, 2001 and a killing of more than 3,000 people inside them by the hijackers who collided two jumbo passenger planes into the buildings.*' If you translate '9.11' into a Korean version literally meaning the italicized part as shown above, your final translation will not likely make the deadline and your effort to be faithful will end up futile.

Translating from a major language to a minor one is usually regarded as easier than translating the other way around because background knowledge in the source text is often shared by the translator and the readers of the target text. Now, let's take 6.25 for example. You now are working on a Korean text about 6.25. You, as a Korean national, easily understand that the three numerals symbolize '*the Korean War provoked by North Korea on June 25, 1950 which killed more than 3 million civilians and soldiers from home and abroad.*' If you translate '6.25' into English or a non-Korean language to mean as has been shown right above, your translation will be well accepted as reader-friendly and therefore marketable.

Text for Translation

1 잘 살고 또 삶의 질을 전반적으로 향상시키는데 있어 실내 주거공간은 매우 중요하다.

⇨ When we want to live well, and generally improve our quality of life, we can benefit quite a lot by **giving attention to** interior living spaces.

2 집이 멋있고 조용해야, 잘 쉴 수 있고 일상의 스트레스를 빨리 해소할 수 있다.

⇨ When we find our home attractive and peaceful, we rest better and recover from our daily stresses more easily.

3 실내주거공간을 개선하는 훌륭하고도 저렴한 방법은 실내에 화분을 놓는 것이다.

⇨ One excellent and relatively inexpensive way to improve our interior spaces is to bring potted plants into our homes or offices.

4 먼저, 식물로 정원을 만들거나, 실내를 꾸미는 방법을 살펴볼 것이다.

⇨ First, we will go over ways that plants can be used to make a garden or decorate a space.

5 둘째, 어떤 식물을 심을 지에 대해 알아볼 것이다.

⇨ Second, we will find out how to prepare plants to live in pots.

6 그런 다음 식물의 생육에 필요한 것들과 관리방법을 알아볼 것이다.

⇨ Next, we will see what plants need to survive and **how to** care for them.

7 마지막으로, 실내에 식물이 있으면 무엇이 좋은가를 설명할 것이다

⇨ Last, we will go over some of the **benefits from** having plants in our interior spaces.

The first decision we need to make is where, and for what reason, we want to put plants in our space. In some cases, the goal is to create an indoor garden that is more or less similar to a natural space outdoors. In these cases, we will likely get a variety of plants of different kinds, sizes and colors; then mix them together. Some plants do best with more or less humidity, some with more or less soil water, and some with more or less sunshine.

8 이러한 다양한 이유로, 어떤 식물은 양지가 좋아 큰 식물로 자라고, 어떤 식물은 큰 식물 아래 음지가 좋아 작은 식물로 자라난다.

⇨ **For all these reasons,** some do better as high plants in full sun, while others do better as shorter plants in the partial or complete shading below the taller plants.

9 갖가지 모양과 크기의 식물을 실내에 두고 싶다면, 그에 걸맞게 다양한 화분을 준비하는 것이 좋다.

⇨ In spaces where there are many plants of different types and sizes, a variety of pots is also a good idea.

10 다양한 질감, 색깔, 모양, 형태의 사기 또는 토기 화분은 실내 정원을 보는 재미를 한층 더해준다.

⇨ The different surface textures, colors, shapes and types of ceramic and earthenware pots add a great deal of additional interest to our gardens.

11 최근에는 플라스틱이나 금속제 화분이 나오고 광섬유로 만든 화분도 나온다.

⇨ In recent years, pots are being **made of** plastic, metal, even fiberglass.

12 그런 화분은 쉽게 구할 수 있고 값도 싸지만, 보다 자연에 가까운 사기나 토기 화분만큼 멋지지 않다.

⇨ While often adequate, and cheap, we find that such pots are not as satisfying or as attractive as the more natural ones.

13 실내정원을 만들기에는 공간이 협소하거나, 특정공간만을 디자인 용도로 쓰고 싶다면, 그에 맞는 크기와 모양의 식물을 둘 수도 있다.

⇨ Where there is not enough space for a garden, or where a certain space has a design function, we may wish to place a certain size and shape of plant in that space.

14 이런 경우, 화분의 주변과 윗 공간을 고려해야 한다.
⇨ **In such cases**, we need to consider the space above and around each pot.

15 가용공간을 알면 어떤 모양의 식물을 키울 수 있을지 알게 된다.
⇨ The volume of space available will suggest the best shape, or growth form, of plant to put there.

16 예를 들면, 널찍한 원형 공간이 있다면, 둥근 공간을 차지하고 관목형태인 야자수 계통의 식물이 좋다.
⇨ For example, a large spherical space would benefit from a round, bushy plant, perhaps one of the palms.

17 반면 높지만 협소한 공간이 있다면, 그에 맞춰 높고 곧장 자라는 대나무 정도가 적합하다.
⇨ **On the other hand**, a high, narrow space in a corner would call for a similarly tall, vertical plant, perhaps a small bamboo.

18 화분 또한 그 식물과 어울리게끔 둥글고 넓적한 것이나 호리호리하고 높은 것을 골라야 할 것이다.
⇨ We should also choose a pot that gives the same impression, for these examples, either round and squat, or slender and tall.

19 식물의 크기와 모양을 정하고 또 그에 걸맞는 모양의 색의 화분도 정했다면 이제는 식물의 잎사귀 모양이나 크기도 정해야 한다.

⇨ After we have chosen the plant size and shape, and selected a pot that matches in shape and color, we might still have some options **as to** the leaf shapes and color of the plant we will use.

20 물론, 대다수 식물이 초록색이지만, 줄기, 잎, 꽃의 색깔은 매우 다양하다.

⇨ Of course, most plants are dark green, but there are many variations in both stem or leaf colors and flower colors.

21 어떤 식물은 꽃이 피지 않는다.

⇨ Some plants **have** no flowers.

양치류   소철   침엽수   솔송나무   낙엽송

Ferns, cycads, and conifers (pines, hemlocks, and larches) are among the larger, non-flowering plants used for potting.

Since conifers are trees, if we use them in our garden or other spaces, they **are likely to** be in the form of the small, carefully cultivated trees called 'bonsai' in Japanese.

When, as in this example, our choices are based on design effects, we may have to put artificial light over the plants, if they are not near a door or window. Plants use mostly chlorophyll, and some other pigments, to capture the energy in light, so they must be exposed to several hours of light each day. Some, like many ferns, need a few hours of indirect light; whereas plants like cacti thrive if exposed to many hours of direct light.

22 푸르스름한 일반 형광등 불빛도 식물의 생장에 좋다. 그러나, 많은 개화 식물은 봄철의 햇살이나 붉은 빛을 쪼여야 꽃을 틔운다.

⇨ The blue-green light of common fluorescent bulbs is good for growing plants, but many flowering plants need spring time exposure to sunlight or red light to bloom.

23 빛과 잎 구멍으로 빨아들이는 공기 외에도, 식물은 토양으로부터 필요한 물질을 흡수한다.
⇨ Aside from light and the air they take in through their leaf openings, plants get all the other things they need from the soil.

Through their roots in the soil, they take up water and with it, the dissolved nutrients they need to grow and develop. Since this is largely a physical process, plants pull more water from the soil and release more vapor from their leaves when temperatures are high. Growth, and most other activity, stops in most plants during cold weather. Once or twice each year, plants should be given extra nutrients. This process is called 'feeding' and either solid or liquid products may be used. Many flowering plants need such special nutrients in the spring to start blooming.

24 화분에서 수년을 자라면, 식물은 토양 유기물질 중 상당부분을 꽃, 줄기, 잎, 뿌리 등 식물의 몸체로 바꾼다.
⇨ After several years in a pot, growing plants will have converted a significant amount of the soil organics into new plant biomass (flowers, stems, leaves, and roots).

For this reason, the top of the plant will clearly be larger, while the amount of soil in the pot will be clearly diminished. Unseen is that the root mass has also greatly increased and may have become too tight (root bound) for the plant to stay healthy. For all these reasons, each plant should be removed from its pot every so often, have its roots trimmed, have its soil replaced, and be re-potted for its next cycle of several years.

25 많은 식물은 정기적으로 물을 주어야 잘 살 수 있다.
⇨ Many plants do best when placed on a watering schedule.

For most plants, in warm weather, once a week is enough if their soil is thoroughly soaked each time. In winter, watering may be reduced to every other week, or even once a month for some plants. Though they can survive with much less, most desert plants do much better when given regular watering. The soil of potted plants should always be well drained. If liquid water stays in the pots after watering, the roots of many plants will be damaged by fungi. If the tops of plants begin wilting, it means that they need watering immediately, or that their roots have been damaged and can no longer take up water.

At this point, we have chosen the spaces and pots, we have bought some plants and know how we are going to provide them with the light they need. Next, we need to get them into our pots. We have chosen pots with a hole in the center of the bottom. This will drain excess water, but it will also release too much soil. From the plant shop, we purchased a sheet of plastic mesh with many small holes in it. Now, we cut a piece of mesh just large enough to cover the bottom of our pot (and the hole). Last, we cover the plastic with a 4-6 cm layer of small stones. Stones of about one centimeter in diameter are preferable.

26 돌은 배수는 돕지만, 흙은 빠져나가지 못하도록 한다.

⇨ This stony layer will pass the draining water, but will **stop the soil from** running out.

Next, we fill the pot with good clean potting soil, leaving 10 to 15 cm of empty space at the top for the plant and its roots. We put in the plant chosen for that pot and adjust the soil until the base of the plant –the part just above the roots – is slightly above the rim of the pot.

27 그런 다음 뿌리에 흙을 덮고, 식물의 밑둥 (뿌리 바로 위 부분)이 화분 끝보다 약간 낮아질 때까지 단단히 눌러준다.

⇨ Then we cover the roots with soil and press it down until the soil is firm and the base of the plant is just below the rim of the pot.

28 자, 이제 골이 생겼으므로 여기에 고인 물이 서서히 흙 속으로 흡수된다.

⇨ Now there is a depression where water may gather and slowly soak down into the soil.

Expressions Review

1 have (instead of 'there is')

2 have (instead of other verbs)

3 give attention to something

4 how to do something

5 for + adjective + reason

6 benefit from something

7 made of something

8 in + adjective + case(s)

9 On the other hand

10 likely to do something

Model Dialogue

Amy: When you hear the word 'Nature,' what comes to mind?

James: "Well, I think about plants, soil, air, clouds and pretty much everything on earth. But I don't really know how to describe Nature. Do you?

Amy: Me, neither. But I know how to care of it. You can protect Nature when you give a little attention to a small rock or a blade of grass which would otherwise easily go unnoticed.

James: Yeah, but for some economic reasons, people destroy Nature. And once destroyed, Nature is not likely to recover soon from the damage.

Amy: People benefit much more from protecting and preserving Mother Nature than from destroying or developing her.

Talking Practice

Now, the class divides into two groups. The two groups of students sit in line facing each other. Each pair of students will talk about the topic using the expressions for 5 minutes. After each talking session is finished, students will move anticlockwise to talk to a new partner for another 5 minutes. Talking Practice ends when students meet their first partner again.

Review Test

▶ Following is part of the main text. Fill the blanks to complete the text (1 point for each blank).

For most plants in warm weather once a 1. _____ is enough if their soil is thoroughly soaked each time. In winter, watering may be reduced to every other week, or even once a month for some plants. Though they can survive with much less, most desert plants do much better when given regular watering. The soil of potted plants should always be well drained. If liquid water stays in the pots after watering, the roots of many plants will be damaged by 2. _____. If the tops of plants begin wilting, it means that they need watering immediately, or that their roots have been damaged and can no longer take up 3. _____.***

At this point, we have chosen the spaces and pots, we have bought some plants and know how we are going to provide them with the light they need. Next, we need to get them into our pots. We have chosen pots with a hole in the center of the bottom. This will drain excess water, but it will also release too much 4. _____. From the plant shop, we purchased a sheet of plastic mesh with many small holes in it. Now, we cut a piece of mesh just large enough to cover the bottom of our pot (and the hole). Last, we cover the plastic with a 4-6 cm layer of small 5. _____. Stones of about one centimeter in diameter are preferable.*****

▶ Translate the following Korean sentences into English (3 points each).

1 최근에는 플라스틱이나 금속제 화분이 나오고 광섬유로 만든 화분도 나온다.

2 집이 멋있고 조용해야, 잘 쉴 수 있고 일상의 스트레스를 빨리 해소할 수 있다.

3 최근에는 플라스틱이나 금속제 화분이 나오고 광섬유로 만든 화분도 나온다.

4 물론, 대다수 식물이 초록색이지만, 줄기, 잎, 꽃의 색깔은 매우 다양하다.

5 어떤 식물은 꽃이 피지 않는다.

Chapter 2

Translation as Storytelling

What is Storytelling?

Storytelling is the noun version of the verb, 'to tell a story.' The emphasis is both on 'story', and on 'telling'. Storytelling is an effort to make a narrative out of numbers, statements, tables, and other more formal written text. The beauty of storytelling is its ability to make information, or message, more reader-friendly. Reader friendliness is one of the most important traits successful translations should have. That is where translation and storytelling meet. Telling is an oral action; it is different from translating, which is mainly a 'writing' act. Thus, the 'telling' aspect of storytelling is about the ease with which messages are conveyed, as if in conversation.

If translation gets into a 'telling' mode we call it 'interpretation', which is a 'telling' act. These days, the information format seems to be divided into two: digital and analog. In the modern digital age, characterized by such digital machines as computers, efficiency is more valued than in the past when informal, face-to-face contact, or analog mode, was the only option. But in the peak of the digital area, people begin to realize the importance of a balance between digital and analogue modes of conveying information.

In translation studies, storytelling has a different name: *naturalness*. Translation is not just about a long list of archaic and technical glossary. Many translation students feel overwhelmed in their first translation class after being given a huge glossary assignment by their teacher. Preparing a glossary list is not a big part of translating. Speaking your own language, I mean, using more natural vocabulary is sometimes much better than cut-and-dried stylized terminology. Just think of the glossary as a supplement to help you tell a story out of the source text. If help is not needed, go ahead on your own! Brown wrote in his book 'Storytelling in Organization', one of the silliest phrases he ever heard was, 'Stop talking and get back to business.' Talking, or telling, could be more important and more serious than business.

In fact, writing this book is also an approach to making a translation book more like a storytelling task. I try to use fewer academic terms in the main text and make a point of including a dialog session at the end of each chapter so that you can express the contents in the translation text through your own vocabulary to your partner(s).

Storytelling, however, should be differentiated from making a story, which is not based on a source text. The translator usually makes a decision whether the story of his or her own making is in line with the source text. Telling a story is not telling a lie. Storytelling is accepted and sometimes recommended out only within a limit. The aspect of storytelling in translation is very clearly observed in film subtitles. I enjoy using movies in translation classrooms because subtitlers try to tell as much story as possible in only a few lines of subtitles. Sometimes students are often found to be excellent story tellers when they are asked to.

Storytelling should be one of the first steps in teaching translation. In interpreting classes as well, it would also be educational to have a storytelling session before note taking classes occur. Many note taking classes tend to emphasize improving the summarizing skills. By telling a story first, students may first be able to decide which information is to be summarized or omitted. In order to become a good story teller, you have first to become a good speaker of the target language, or mostly in this classroom, the Korean language. Because of the storytelling aspect of translation, the personality of the translator reveals itself, whether intended or not, through the translated versions. The translator as a storyteller tells his/her own story through the mouth of the author.

Text for Translation

1 보통 '보건'하면 아플 때 치료 받는 것쯤으로 생각한다.
⇨ For many, health only means getting medical treatment when they are sick.

Let's consider another approach - a strategy for optimum health. We want to manage some important daily activities to stay as healthy and happy as possible, and in particular, to reduce the amount of time we are sick. Before we go into specific details, we need to learn a bit about how our bodies manage our internal resources: nutrients, fiber, water, and energy. Our bodies are complex systems in which biological, chemical, and physical components are carefully coordinated.

2 인체는 에너지가 있어야 움직일 수 있고 자주 정비도 해주어야 한다. 마치 기계처럼 말이다.

⇨ The human body **requires** energy to do work and needs frequent maintenance – as machines do.

Unlike most machines, our body comes with its own operating system (OS). Our OS is able to determine what needs to be done to ensure survival, when to make changes or avoid them, and how to manage body resources in time and space. At all times, the OS must provide nutrition and energy to all the cells in our body.

3 운영체제는 인체의 체액을 정화하고 동시에 죽거나, 손상되거나 불필요해진 세포를 제거하고 또 새로 만들어낸다.

⇨ It also cleanses body fluids, while it removes and replaces cells that are dead, damaged, or no longer needed.

4 오늘 논의에서 중요한 것은 바로 운영체제는 환경변화를 감지하고 그에 맞게 반응한다는 점이다.

⇨ Very important to our discussion, is that the OS is able to sense changing conditions and **respond to** them. If we begin a new exercise program, our muscles, lungs, heart, and blood vessels must be upgraded, and our bones strengthened to support the stronger muscles. If we go to a hot place, or the weather heats up, the OS will cause blood vessels near the skin to accept more blood flow and sweat glands to become very active, to cool our bodies. Keeping interior conditions stable when exterior conditions are changing, and reacting to other kinds of challenges, use a lot of resources.

5 자원은 항상 한정돼 있으므로 운영체제는 활동 별로 우선순위를 매긴다.
⇨ Because resources are always limited, the OS is able to **give priority to** some actions, and delay others.

In cold weather, more warm blood is directed away from the skin to the brain and heart. If necessary, the OS will sacrifice the nose, ears or fingers, to keep the brain and heart in good condition.

6 밤에 술을 마시면 간은 인체로부터 독소를 제거하고 그로 인한 피해를 복구하기 위해 열심히 일할 것이다.
⇨ If we drink alcohol one night, the liver will be working hard to clear this damaging toxin from our bodies and repair **the damage it has done**.

We are much more likely to get sick if we place many demands on the OS at the same time. The qualities of our other physical and mental functions are also diminished.

All this leads us to the first idea for optimum health. We need to pay attention when we do things that put a lot of demands on our bodies and compensate.

7 과도한 부담의 예로, 특히 고기를 곁들인 과식, 소금, 카페인, 알코올, 약물의 과다섭취를 들 수 있다.

⇨ Examples of such demands might include heavy meals – particularly with meat – excessive use of salt, caffeine, alcohol, and medical drugs.

We need to be wary of extended exposure to cold water, sun, and strong wind. Also important are sickness and sustained stresses.

When our bodies are dealing with such demands, we need to spend some time relaxing or resting, to give our OS the chance to get us back in good condition.

8 이럴 때는 소식하고, 희석된 과일쥬스를 마시며 카페인이나 알코올섭취를 피하면서, 피곤할 경우 낮잠을 자야 한다.

⇨ These are times to eat lightly, drink diluted fruit juices, avoid caffeine and alcohol, and nap **if needed**.

The second idea for optimum health is an extension of the first. Give high value to rest and, in particular, to sleep at night. When we sleep, and stop most of our usual activities, the OS is able to redirect large amounts of resources to cleaning, restoring, and altering our bodies.

9 따라서 숙면은 선택이 아닌 필수사항이다.
⇨ For this reason, high quality sleep is **not at all** optional.

We can see this clearly, if we consider the symptoms of insufficient nightly sleep. For sure, we can expect to gain fat. Other symptoms may include general weakness, poor liver and bowel^장 function, increased infections, muddy thinking, paranoia^{편집증} and depression^{우울증}.

10 잠을 충분히 자두면 이런 증상들이 해소되고, 다시 좋은 컨디션을 회복하게 된다.
⇨ When we get adequate sleep, these symptoms reverse, and we begin to feel good again.

11 최적 수면시간은 사람마다 다른데. 일반적으로 6 내지 9 시간 사이이며 평균8시간이다.
⇨ The amount of sleep needed for optimum health varies, but generally **ranges from** 6-9 hours per night, with 8 hours being adequate for most people.

When we are sick or depressed, we need a great deal more sleep. Babies and young children, who are growing very rapidly, need a lot of sleep. A useful thing to know is that when we miss sleep, we can largely make it up later by sleeping longer. If we must go several days with too little sleep, we may spend our weekends sleeping, as many people do. It is easy to determine if our sleep is adequate.

12 잠을 푹 자면, 깰 때도 자연스럽고, 일어나서도 힘이 넘치고 기분이 상쾌하다.

⇨ When it is, we wake up automatically, we feel energetic, and the world seems a cheerful place.

The third idea for optimum health is managing our body fat. There is a lot of information these days that shows that body fat levels above 30% of our body mass may lead to many conditions that result in poor health.

13 체지방이 너무 적어도 문제다.

⇨ Too little body fat is also not healthy.

Athletes may have around 15% fat or a little less, but most people should aim for low to mid-20s.

14 현대인들에게, 25%로 체지방을 줄이고 그것을 유지하기란 결코 쉽지 않다.

⇨ In modern times, reaching and maintaining 25% body fat can be challenging.

This will require adequate sleep, an excellent diet, and frequent exercise.

15 식단이란 우리가 먹고 마시는 모든 음식물을 일컫는다.

⇨ Our diet is everything that we eat and drink.

From our food and drink, we take water, fiber, and nutrients. These provide the OS with all the resources it needs to operate our bodies.

16 고품질의 식단이 되려면 여러 가지 요건을 충족시켜야 한다.
⇨ A high quality diet requires attention to several factors.

First, the things in our diet need to be clean - **free of** artificial fertilizers and pesticides. In the USA, when food is labeled 'organic' it is certifiably clean in this sense. Next, using local produce is superior.

17 우리 고장의 과일과 채소는 긴 운송시간을 견딜 필요가 없으므로 익었을 때 바로 수확된 것을 사먹을 수 있다.
⇨ Local fruits and vegetables don't need to travel far, so they can be picked, sold, and eaten when they are ripe.

18 따라서 영양도 만점, 맛도 만점이다.
⇨ This makes them **as nutritious and delicious as possible**.

There are ways of handling our diet that can make good foods work even better. Eat lightly, several times a day. If we eat irregular e.g., heavy meals late at night, we can expect poor digestion and unusual weight gains. Use a lot of fruits and vegetables in your diet, both for fiber and nutrients; use starchy vegetables and grains in moderation. We need good oils in our diet, and coconut oil is good for cooking. Also helpful are organic olive oil (eaten uncooked) and a clean source of omega 3 (often fish oils).

Clean animal protein is fine, but provides little fiber and is harder to digest.

19 영양 보강제는 여러모로 건강에 좋다.
⇨ Nutrient supplements can be helpful **in many ways**.

These days we also need to consider the water we drink. If possible, it is best to use a quality home water purifier to assure clean water for drinking and cooking. It is best to get as much water as possible from juicy fruits and vegetables in our diet. Pure water has very little of the minerals we need. Be aware that caffeine, alcohol, and many drugs cause our bodies to release water, which drains our water-soluble vitamins. Finally, we must be aware of the quality of the water that we drink, or in which we swim.

Expressions Review

1 require (instead of 'have to do' or 'in order to do')

2 give priority to

3 respond to

4 do damage[harm]

5 if needed

6 not at all

7 range from somewhere to somewhere

8 free of

9 as + adjective[advervb] + as + past particle

10 in many ways

Model Dialogue

Amy: These days, there is a lot of talk about genetically modified food, or GM food, for short.

James: Yeah, GM food ranges from GM crops to GM meat. Health experts say we should avoid GM food because it does damage to our health in many ways.

Amy: But some people say GM food is not harmful at all. They say the international community should respond to the famine problem in the third world by creating more GM crops.

James: They can make their case only if the GM food proves not as harmful as imagined.

Amy: Strict monitoring of food distribution system is required more than ever before if we want our diet free of hazardous substances.

Talking Practice

Now, the class divides into two groups. The two groups of students sit in line facing each other. Each pair of students will talk about the topic using the expressions for 5 minutes. After each talking session is finished, students will move anticlockwise to talk to a new partner for another 5 minutes. Talking Practice ends when students meet their first partner again.

Review Test

▶ Following is part of the main text. Fill the blanks to complete the text (1 point for each blank).

When we are sick or depressed, we need a great deal more sleep. Babies and young children, who are growing very rapidly, need a lot of sleep. A useful thing to know is that when we miss sleep, we can largely make it up later by sleeping longer. If we must go several days with too little sleep, we may spend our 1. _____ sleeping, as many people do. It is easy to determine if our sleep is adequate..***

Examples of such demands might include heavy meals – particularly with 2. _____ – excessive use of salt, caffeine, alcohol, and medical drugs.

We need to be wary of extended exposure to cold water, sun, and strong wind. Also important are sickness and sustained stresses. When our bodies

are dealing with such demands, we need to spend some time relaxing or resting, to give our OS the chance to get us back in good 3._____.
***

The amount of sleep needed for optimum health varies, but generally ranges from 6-9 hours per night, with 4. _____ being adequate for most 5. _____.

▶ Translate the following Korean sentences into English (3 points each).

1 영양 보강제는 여러모로 건강에 좋다.

2 잠을 충분히 자두면 이런 증상들이 해소되고, 다시 좋은 컨디션을 회복하게 된다

3 보통 '보건'하면 아플 때 치료 받는 것쯤으로 생각한다

4 인체는 에너지가 있어야 움직일 수 있고 자주 정비도 해주어야 한다. 마치 기계처럼 말이다.

5 우리 고장의 과일과 채소는 긴 운송시간을 견딜 필요가 없으므로 익었을 때 바로 수확된 것을 사먹을 수 있다.

Chapter 3

Translation as Economy of Language

Shorter is Better

Translation often means a race against time because almost every translation task has its deadline, a point in time for the translator to deliver his translation to those who have ordered it. The problem about deadlines is that they are fast sneaking upon you. Translations should be short because readers do not like the idea of reading thick books. Making a shorter translation requires a lot of techniques which will be explained later in this book. This chapter explains why people want to communicate in a more economic way and how. And I don't think the first question of why is that difficult to answer. Communication is a form of human behavior, and also that of many other animals, and even plants. Humans instinctively want their behaviors to be more efficient because by doing so, they can save energy and time for other more useful purposes.

The question of 'how' is more succinctly answered by Grice, who formulated principles about how humans communicate efficiently, and effectively as well. Those principles are called 'Grice's Cooperative Principles' and they do not necessarily sound new. They are:

1. About Quantity of Discourse
   a) Only as much as needed
   b) Never more than needed
2. About Quality
   a) Only contents regarded as true
   b) Never ungrounded contents
3. About Relevance
   a) Make it relevant
4. About Manner
   a) Make is precise
   b) Make it unequivocal
   c) Make it simple
   d) Make it reasonable

They are not a sophisticated set of rules to memorize for a successful communication to happen. They are just a part of our everyday language habits. But in real practice these four principles are much easier said than done. Let's take Principle No.4 about "Manner" which requires us to 'Make it simple'. How could we make the text in question simple? How simple is simple enough? Which does 'simple' necessarily mean, the length of a sentence, the number of words, or the whole text? The questions go on and on. If questions are endless for just one specific principle, how many will there be for all four principles and their subordinate rules? Thus, the translator should make a decision on whether Grice would have liked his translation. That's why we call the translator a decision maker. They have to make decisions at a word level, phrasal level, sentence level, and finally text level. And one decision at one level often contradicts another one at a different level.

Translation is often a struggle to fit the source text into a confined space. Even without the time constraint, space still acts as another constraint for the translator. Suppose you are a very fast translator and finish the translating task a few days ahead of the deadline but you have made your translation twice as long as the original. Can you still consider yourself a success? The answer is an absolute 'no'. This means that the translator works under two constraints working against him at the same time: time and space. A form of translation under an extreme time constraint is 'simultaneous interpretation.' A form of translation under an extreme space constraint is 'subtitling'. The remaining forms of translation are inbetween. Film subtitles are often valued as quite a useful tool for students to understand the constraints by giving them an opportunity to work under an extreme space limit. If subtitling task is coupled with dubbing task, it provides the students with a good opportunity to work under both time and space limits.

Text for Today

1 선진국에 사는 사람들은 대개 물의 소중함을 잘 모른다.
⇨ Most often, in developed countries, we **take** water **for granted.**

2 물은 필요할 때면 언제나 구할 수 있는 것으로 생각할 정도다.

⇨ We have **come to** expect clean water whenever we need_it.

In many countries around the world, the reality is that water is merely adequate for present needs, and inadequate for future needs.

People only last a few days without water, and survival requires several liters of water per day. The exact amount depends on the heat and level of physical activity.

3 가정에서 물의 용도는 식수, 요리 그리고 세척 등이다.

⇨ At home, we use water for drinking, cooking, and sanitation.

Employees at businesses do the same, but also use water for preparing and cleaning their products, diluting pollutants, cooling, and generating electricity. In rural areas, personal use is tiny compared to the amount used for irrigation of crops. Common estimates are that agriculture uses about 70% of overall water use in many countries.

4 이스라엘 같은 물 부족 국가에서는 농부들이 1리터의 물에서 한 톨이라도 더 많은 작물을 생산하려고 안간힘을 쓴다.

⇨ In a few places, such as Israel, scarcity has **forced farmers to be** much more efficient in how much they can produce from each liter.

There are huge differences in how water is used in undeveloped, developing, and well-developed countries. In many parts of the world, survival and minimal cleanliness is the best case.

5 물은 강, 호수, 우물에서 직접 떠서 그것도 때론 먼 거리를 짊어지고 와야 한다.

⇨ Water is carried from rivers, lakes, or wells to homes by hand, often over long distances.

This takes a lot of time and energy that cannot be used for other things. It also limits how much water can be used for agriculture. By contrast, those in highly developed countries have water on tap in their homes, and interior flush toilets. Our bodies, possessions, and homes can be kept clean easily. In those places where people have many possessions, a lot of water may be used to clean cars and other outdoor equipment, to water lawns, and to grow ornamental plants in public parks.

6 이상은 물의 직접적인 용도들이다.

⇨ These are all direct uses.

Water also plays some very important **indirect** roles in modern societies. A major role is transportation of raw and finished goods. The cheapest way to transport large amounts of goods over long distances is by water, most often in barges, container ships, or tankers. Many cities and industries still use water to wash away and dilute harmful wastes, though this is now largely unacceptable. In addition, water plays a huge role supporting natural areas with essential services to us all.

7 물은 또한 날씨와 기후에도 중대한 영향을 미친다.

⇨ Water is also the most important factor in our weather and climate.

There are lifeless, waterless planets where weather exists, but their barren surfaces and their types of weather are nothing at all like those found in the rich landscape of our planet.

8 기후란, 장기간 계속되는 날씨의 패턴을 말한다.

⇨ Climate is simply weather considered **over long periods of time**.

The weather we experience each day is created by a combination of air movement, temperature, and rainfall.

9 엄청난 양의 열을 흡수, 이동, 방출하는 물의 독특한 능력이 날씨를 만든다.

⇨ The uniquely high capacity of water to absorb, move, and release large amounts of heat is the main driver of our weather.

Thus, how water distributes heat locally causes specific areas to be cold or hot, wet or dry, and windy or calm. In addition to these roles, water is the dominant force shaping the world we see. The surface topography^{지형} of our planet is weathered by exposure to sunlight, temperature extremes, chemicals, and erosion by wind and water. Erosion by moving water has the greatest effect. As water moves stones, sand, and smaller soil particles from land into bodies of water, river channels, lakes, and even ocean basins, these bodies are filled with sedimentation.^(침전물) This alters the surface of dry land as well as the underwater bottoms.

10 수면의 상승과 하강은 우리가 보는 우리가 살아가는 땅 모양을 만든다.

⇨ Water also **affects** how much land we see and live on, simply by rising and falling.

During the ice ages, sea levels dropped as water evaporated from oceans and precipitated onto inland glaciers. This exposed shallow sea bottoms around most continents and islands. During global warming, ice melts and these same coastal areas are covered by water.

Last in our list of uses for water, is water's many cultural impacts. Water often plays important roles in rituals of major religions, particularly those of Hinduism, Christianity, and Islam, as well as in many shamanistic^(무속의) or pagan^(이단의) religions.

11 심지어 사진, 시, 문학, 건축 등 예술분야에 있어서도 물의 영향력은 대단하다.

⇨ Even in our art: photography, poetry, literature and architecture, water has had unique influences.

There are few people unattracted by lovely water gardens or riverside parks.

Now let's consider how people in developing and developed countries

have come to be served by water. Where resources are sufficient, three different kinds of water services are provided. The first of these deals with water supply. Those concerned with water supply locate sufficient quantities of water to satisfy the need of those they serve. Typically, this requires transportation and storage of large amounts of water, often using dams and reservoirs. Recently, a new concern of those in water supply is that sufficient water remains in natural waterways so that **flora and fauna** there remain healthy.
<small>동식물</small>

Another service is water drainage.

12 배수에 있어서 가장 중요한 것은 홍수통제다.

⇨ The first task of water drainage is usually flood control. Incoming water may be limited in various ways, such as with dikes or levees, while excess water is conducted safely outside the target areas.

13 배수가 잘 돼야 공중보건과 질병통제가 쉬워진다.

⇨ Water drainage also **plays a** large **part in** public sanitation and disease control.

By diverting animal and human wastes away from habitations, bad odors and sanitation are much improved.

14 질병통제가 잘 되려면, 오폐수가 식수로 유입되지 않도록 막아야 하고, 질병을 옮기는 생물들이 주로 서식하는 주변의 습지를 건조시켜 없애야 한다.

⇨ Disease control **results from** keeping wastewater out of the drinking supply, and from drying up nearby wetlands where organisms that harbor diseases live.

The third major service is water treatment. Before water can be used by people, it must be of high quality: free of disease-causing organisms, natural poisons (such as) and industrial or agricultural pollutants. For this purpose, special water treatment plants are built and operated to provide a continuous supply of clean, safe water. Likewise, because the water is often highly degraded after use, it must be treated again before it is discharged. If it is not, it will not only degrade the natural environment, but also poison the people who attempt to use the same water as it flows downstream.

15 이렇게 중요한 물 관련 서비스를 공급하려면 돈이 많이 든다.
⇨ Provision of these critical water services **comes at a** high **price.**

Water treatment plants are not cheap. Neither are the projects by which huge water pipes are made to run hundreds of miles from water sources to the cities that they serve. Once there, a maze of smaller and smaller pipes thousands of miles long moves the water from the supply areas into individual homes and businesses. After the water is used, a mirror image network of small waste water pipes becomes larger and larger until they reach treatment plants.

16 이러한 일을 하는 수도관, 양수기, 오폐수 처리시설 등 모든 시설을

통칭하여 "수자원 인프라"라고 부른다.

⇨ All the equipment needed to do these things: pipes, pumps, treatment plants and so on, are collectively called the water services infrastructure.

The presence of water limits where people and their cities can occur, and always has. The expense of establishing effective infrastructure is a huge collective investment. All this means that changes in the water supply can have catastrophic impacts on an area. We are now seeing shifts in rainfall patterns thought to be related to global warming. This may be true, but such shifts are well known by those who study ancient climates.

A number of ancient civilizations, among them the Mesopotamians, the Maya and several smaller cultures in what is now the southwestern USA, are thought to have fallen due to failure of rainfall patterns in their areas. What we are seeing is not new, except to us.

It is also true that while some areas will become drier, others will become wetter.

17 당장 걱정스러운 것은 인간이 물을 오용하고 남용한다는 점이다.

⇨ A more immediate concern is our own misuse and waste of water.

In spite of its extreme value for the survival of our global society, water is given a monetary value so low that there is no reason not to waste it. It is well known that conservation measures can reduce water use in many places by as much as 30% without affecting quality of life much at all. Furthermore, conservation programs are cheap and effective.

18 그럼에도 불구하고, 절수 정책을 시행하는 국가는 거의 없다.
⇨ Even so, very few governments maintain conservation programs.

There are much better ways to irrigate crops, but few governments require these methods. Water hungry crops are still being grown in near-deserts with transported water. Around the world, aquifers are still being used faster than they can recharge.

19 정말로, 우리들은 아직도 문제의 심각성을 인식하지 못하고 있다.
⇨ Clearly, we haven't **gotten the message**.

20 의지만 있다면, 많은 기술이나 방법을 이용해 물을 아낄 수 있다.
⇨ Many promising technologies and methods will **allow us to use** water more efficiently, if we have the desire to do so.

It appears that for many people in many regions, time has almost run out.

21 물이 비교적 넉넉한 곳에 사는 사람들이 물 부족으로 생존의 위기에 처한 사람들을 도와줄지는 관연 두고 볼 일이다.
⇨ **It remains to be seen** if those in wetter areas can do anything to assist those who are at risk of perishing in the drier areas.

1 take something for granted

2 come to do something

3 force somebody to do something

4 affect (in a negative sense)

5 play a role in something

6 result from something

7 come at a price

8 get the message

9 allow somebody to do something

10 It remains to be seen

Model Dialogue

Amy: We humans cannot live without water.

James: Water allows us to do many different things and our bodies are more than 70% water. Weather results mostly from water. Water played a major role in developing human civilizations.

Amy: But many people take water for granted such that there's even an expression in Korean, 'to use something like water', which means, 'use something wastefully.'

James: People should know that water comes at a price- at a pretty high price! If water authorities charge a high price for water, then people will get the message.

Amy: But compared to those of other countries, water comes at a much lower price in our country.

James: So the government is taking a lot of measures to conserve water resources. It remains to be seen whether those measures will prove successful in making people come to realize the severity of water shortages.

Talking Practice

Now, the class divides into two groups. The two groups of students sit in line facing each other. Each pair of students will talk about the topic using the expressions for 5 minutes. After each talking session is finished, students will move anticlockwise to talk to a new partner for another 5 minutes. Talking Practice ends when students meet their first partner again.

Review Test

▶ Following is part of the main text. Fill the blanks to complete the text (1 point for each blank).

Employees at businesses do the same, but also use water for preparing and cleaning their products, diluting pollutants, cooling, and generating electricity. In rural areas, personal use is tiny compared to the amount used for 1. _____ of crops. Common estimates are that agriculture uses about 2. _____ of overall water use in many countries.***

Water also plays some very important indirect roles in modern societies. A major role is 3. _____ of raw and finished goods. The cheapest way to transport large amounts of goods over long distances is by water, most often in barges, container ships, or 4. _____. Many cities and industries still use water to wash away and dilute harmful wastes, though this is now largely 5. _____. In addition, water plays a huge role supporting natural areas with essential services to us all.***

▶ Translate the following Korean sentences into English (3 points each).

1 물은 필요할 때면 언제나 구할 수 있는 것으로 생각할 정도다.

2 이상은 물의 직접적인 용도들이다.

3 이렇게 중요한 물 관련 서비스를 공급하려면 돈이 많이 든다.

4 질병통제가 잘 되려면, 오폐수가 식수로 유입되지 않도록 막아야 하고, 질병을 옮기는 생물들이 주로 서식하는 주변의 습지를 건조시켜 없애야 한다.

5 그럼에도 불구하고, 절수 정책을 시행하는 국가는 거의 없다.

Chapter 4

Translators as Future Leaders

Leader is a Translator

Translation is a form of communication involving more than two languages. As we have discussed in previous chapters, successful translation requires world knowledge, proficiency in both source and target language and knowhow of delivering the message in an economic and efficient way. Consequently, the characteristics required of good translators are also some of the essential traits required in a good leader. First of all, a good leader has to be a good communicator, or a good storyteller, which we have discussed in Chapter 3. In modern times, a generalist CEO is valued more than her specialist counterpart. Knowing a little bit of everything works better in solving real-life problems and forming a future vision than knowing everything of a little bit. That's why we call the highest ranking soldiers 'generals', not 'specialists.'

The Korean government is beginning to demand its new employees to have a broader knowledge base, rather than to simply memorize some laws and contents of a handful of exam-oriented books. Some of government-administered exams which have tested a 'limited knowledge' are fast becoming things of the past. Among them is the Diplomats Exams for recruiting young professional diplomats, which is administered by the Ministry of Trade and Foreign Affairs of Korea. Instead, the Diplomats' Academy will promote the education of future diplomats based on a broad knowledge of trade and world affairs. Translation students will have a better chance of getting admitted to the school because knowledge of trade and world affairs are one of the most basic tools required for a good translator. Another case in point is Korea's Bar Exam which tests the knowledge required for becoming a lawyer. The exam will be replaced with education at law schools. Getting admitted to one of the law schools will most likely, if not definitely, mean becoming a lawyer. Furthermore, medical schools recruit their students from a much broader student base than in the past, when only graduates of undergraduate medical schools were almost automatically admitted. Why have Korea's major exams been dismissed in favor of formal education, as seen in the cases of high-ranking government employees, lawyers, diplomats and doctors?

The reason is simple: future leaders, even specialists, need more, much more background knowledge than ever before. This trend will become more evident as time goes by.

Japan, the long-time second largest economic powerhouse in the world, replaced only recently by China, became so primarily because of its open door policy, begun about 150 years ago. This act of widely opening Japan's doors to the rest of the world is more commonly known as the Meiji Reform.

What is the Reform about? What does it mean by '*opening its doors*'? As a result of Japan's open door policy, they were able to translate more foreign books on politics, economy, society and culture, which are the four main categories of translation. In a nutshell, through the quick and diligent translation of foreign books, they came to know what was going on in the outside world.

A good leader has to have a more balanced view on things happening both at home and abroad. And based on that view, he must develop a future vision on when, how and where to take his organization to lead it and help it prosper. A good translator takes advantage of his ability to translate by becoming the first to know what is happening abroad, and becoming the first to interpret and deliver it to the members of his organization. Students must understand that translation is a trait, not a skill to earn a living as a profession. That is why I place the chapter on translation techniques towards the end of this book. By understanding the true nature of translation, students will gain an insight into translation, thus sidestepping any erroneous first impressions about one of the oldest practices and professions of mankind

Text for Translation

1 기독교 신자들은 이 세상과 모든 생물은 하느님이 직접 만들었다고 믿는다.

⇨ Many Christians **believe** that God directly created our world and all the **living things** found in and on it.

The most conservative, often called fundamentalist,^{골수} Christians believe that creation occurred in a single event at the beginning of Earth's existence.

2 진화론에서는 생물의 종은 오랜 시간 동안 서서히 변화하여 다른 생물 종으로 변화한다고 설명한다.

⇨ Evolutionary theory is an **attempt to** describe how biological species change **over time**, to become new species.

Because evolution is thought by scientists to occur over millions of years, this theory became threatening.

To defend their beliefs, some fundamentalist Christians assert that because God exists, and because God directly created our world and the living things in it, then the scientific theory of evolution must be false. Here, we will talk about those creation theories that insist that evolution must be false because it goes against the creation passage in The Holy Bible.

3 제임스판 개신교 성경을 보면 하느님이 세상과 모든 생물을 만드는 데는 6일이 걸렸다고 나온다.

⇨ In the St. James version of the Protestant Christian Bible, creation of the planet and the living things on it **took** six days.

We will call this the first of three beliefs that must be true if this fundamentalist version of creation theory is to be considered true. If this assumption were true, we would expect the ages of the rocks on our world to be similar to the ages of the preserved remains () of the living things.

4 즉, 모든 것이 한날 한시에 만들어졌다면, 돌과 생물의 흔적인 화석은 어디서 발견되든지 모두 나이가 같을 것이다.

⇨ That is, if they were all created at the same time, then the dates^{연대} associated with rocks or fossils, **no matter where** they occur, should be the same.

A great deal of data shows that this is not true.

5 지표면에서 발견된 암석 중 가장 오래된 것은 과학적 방법으로 추정 했을 때 약 38억 년 전에 생성된 것이다.

⇨ The oldest stones at the surface of our planet **have been dated** (their age has been determined scientifically) at about 3.8 billion years old.

The oldest recognizable remains of Life (probably ancient bacteria) have been dated to roughly 3.2 billion years ago. More importantly, fossils of many larger forms of Life (sea animals, plants, dinosaurs and other animals clearly not living today) have been dated at ages from hundreds of millions, to tens of millions, of years or less.

6 요는, 우리가 아는 어떤 단세포 생물보다도 앞서 지구는 존재하고 있었으며 단세포 생물보다 훨씬 후에야 인간을 비롯한 덩치 큰 생물이 나타났다.

⇨ **The point is** that the planet existed long before any single-celled life **that we know of,** and that single cells existed long before larger **life forms,** including us.

This means that, if the scientific dating is correct, then the first part of the Bible cannot be considered an exact statement of historical fact. As some have said, that part of the Bible might best be considered a creation myth recorded by the ancestors of Christians to preserve important moral lessons for later followers.

Predictably, fundamentalist creationists saw the dating process as a critical part of this conclusion. Many have attacked scientific dating with great enthusiasm and creativity, but have chosen to miss the big picture. It is true that each method for dating ancient fossils or other remains has weaknesses. In fact, dating gives an age for each remain with an error factor that may range from hundreds of years to millions of years (for example, a roof tile might have an age of 2000 +/- 200 years).

7 그렇다 하더라도, 과학자들이 이러한 기술을 신봉하는 데에는 네 가지 이유가 있다.

⇨ **Even so**, there are four reasons why scientists **have confidence in** using such techniques.

8 첫째, 연대측정방법은 여러 가지가 있고 모두 나름대로의 장단점이
있다.

⇨ First, there are many <u>dating techniques</u>, each with its own **strengths
and weaknesses**.
연대측정술 (above "dating techniques") / 장점 (above "strengths") / 단점 (above "weaknesses")

This means that several methods are usually available by which to date
the same object. The results won't be the same, but if they are similar,
the numbers are considered reasonable. Second, most of the important
dates are determined by more than one person or lab. If the results are
similar, again, the numbers are considered reasonable. Third, these
techniques are continually being refined so that the uncertainty is reduced,
and confidence in the results increased. Fourth, for things of great
importance, there have been many datings so that confidence in the results
is very high.

합리적 (above "reasonable")

9 이러한 사실들을 종합해 볼 때, 현대의 연대측정과학은 신뢰성이 있
다고 판단할 수 있다.

⇨ **Putting these facts together,** this means that the results from modern
dating techniques can be believed.

The second belief often cited by fundamentalist creationists, is that God
directly created all living things at the same time. If this were true, there
should be no evolutionary sequences showing gradual change in related
groups of species over significant periods. In this case, not all the
differences would be related, they would simply be as God created them,

and all remains should be about the same age.

10 이것은 사실이 아니다.
= true

⇨ This is not **the case**.

Using the same dating methods we just discussed, many lines of progressive change in body characters within groups of related species, have been shown to occur over millions of years and longer.

There are also many cases where large groups of related animals have evolved and then gone extinct - disappeared completely (dinosaurs are the best known).

11 단 한번의 창조로 모든 것이 만들어졌다는 주장은 많은 정교한 과학적 데이터에 의해 입증되지 않는다.

⇨ Again, **it is very clear that** a single creation event is not supported by a very large body of high quality scientific data.

A third belief used by fundamentalist creationists to argue their **case**
논리

is not stated in The Bible. Using descriptions of family lines given in certain parts of The Bible, some biblical scholars have estimated that the age of the Earth since Creation is only 11,000-13,000 years old. (Earlier, less careful estimates were less than 7000 years.) These numbers are based on the life spans of those ancestral Christians reported in The Bible. If this belief were true, we would expect no objects, neither rocks nor fossils, to be older than roughly 15,000 years. In fact, there are many, many examples of rocks and fossils much older than 15,000 years, so this belief cannot be true.

🔟2️⃣ 우리가 만일 신앙심이 돈독하고 상당한 지적 수준을 갖춘 기독교인이라면 이런 것들을 어떻게 설명해야 할 것인가?

⇨ If we **take the viewpoint of** a deeply religious and reasonably
= understand
intelligent Christian, what should we **make of** this?

Must we disbelieve Creationism altogether, thus challenging the foundation of our faith? In fact, there are other creation theories that don't
반대하다
oppose the theory of evolution. Instead of clinging fanatically to unsupported beliefs, people doing such work are **making an effort to**
진보성향의
include modern science within progressive creation theories and still retain their Christian beliefs.

I suggest that there is one other thing modern Christians might do. They could search for an ideological space where science and Christian religion might coexist without conflict. Is there such a space? Yes, there is, and it is well known to many scientists. There is a gap in the scientific explanation of the origin of Life. To be exact, evolution is a theory that seeks to explain how species change over time.

Models of the early Earth suggest that conditions there were so ferociously dangerous that no form of life we can imagine could have survived. In half a billion years or so, indications of Life do appear.

1️⃣3️⃣ 생물에 변화가 있으려면, 애당초 생물 자체가 존재해야 하나, 분명이

어떤 생명도 존재하지 않았던 때가 있었을 것이다.

⇨ For changes in life to occur, there must be life, and there was clearly a time when there was none.

14 한마디로 우리는 생명체가 어떻게 출현했는지는 알 수 없다.

⇨ **In a nutshell**, we just don't know how Life started.

First, there was no Life, and then there was. There is an old theory, called <u>spontaneous generation</u> 자연발생설 of Life (worms and larvae 유충 arise from mud), that was ridiculed out of existence some centuries ago. Even so, there must have been a time when the first living thing began to differ from its physical environment.

If I were a modern Christian, looking for a way to reaffirm my faith in creation, and to avoid being concerned about science generally, or evolution in particular, I would envision the hand of God in this gap.

15 과학과 종교는 똑같이 중요하다고 해야 할 것이다.

⇨ Here, it is **safe to say**, scientific theories and religious beliefs have the same weight.

Expressions Review

1 make of something

2 It is safe to say that …

3 in a nutshell

4 For somebody to do something

5 It is clear that···

6 It is not the case

7 strengths and weaknesses

8 putting ···. together

9 make an effort to do something

10 take a viewpoint of somebody [one's viewpoint]

Model Dialogue

Amy: Which do you think came first: the chicken or the egg?

James: I am a firm believer in creationism. So the answer is the chicken. Every living thing should come from its mother.

Amy: Hmm, it's hard for me to take your viewpoint. Eggs must have come first. Eggs are much simpler and smaller than hens, which mean eggs must have been easier to come into existence. In a nutshell, I'm an evolutionist.

James: Many scientists have made futile efforts to prove which theory is right. Each theory has its own strengths and weaknesses.

Amy: Putting those two opposing views together, it might be safe to say that some are created and others are born.

James: So now it's clear that you've made a third theory- a Theory of Life!

Talking Practice

Now, the class divides into two groups. The two groups of students sit in line facing each other. Each pair of students will talk about the topic using the expressions for 5 minutes. After each talking session is finished, students will move anticlockwise to talk to a new partner for another 5 minutes. Talking Practice ends when students meet their first partner again.

Review Test

▶ Following is part of the main text. Fill the blanks to complete the text (1 point for each blank).

The oldest recognizable remains of Life (probably ancient bacteria) have been dated to roughly 1. _____ ago. More importantly, fossils of many larger forms of Life (sea animals, plants, 2. _____ and other animals clearly not living today) have been dated at ages from hundreds of millions, to tens of millions, of years or less.***

The point is that the planet existed long before any single-celled life that we know of, and that single cells existed long before larger life forms, including 3. ___. This means that, if the scientific dating is correct, then the first part of the Bible cannot be considered an exact statement of historical fact. As some have said, that part of the Bible might best be considered a creation 4. ___ recorded by the ancestors of Christians to preserve important moral lessons for later 5. _____.***

▶ Translate the following Korean sentences into English
   (3 points each).

1 지표면에서 발견된 암석 중 가장 오래된 것은 과학적 방법으로 추정했을 때 약 38억년 전에 생성된 것이다.

2 우리가 만일 신앙심이 돈독하고 상당한 지적 수준을 갖춘 기독교인이라면 이런 것들을 어떻게 설명해야 할 것인가?

3 기독교 신자들은 이 세상과 모든 생물은 하느님이 직접 만들었다고 믿는다.

4 그렇다 하더라도, 과학자들이 이러한 기술을 신봉하는 데에는 네 가지 이유가 있다.

5 이것은 사실이 아니다.

Chapter 5   Translation and its Future

The Future Looks Bright

The world is getting smaller with the advent of the internet and the advance of science and technology, which move people and goods faster and more safely at lower costs. The demand for higher-quality translation also goes up with this development. Translation is an integral part of doing successful business, research, and even seeking personal pleasure. Some might say the role traditionally played by human translators would be done by machines with the advent of efficient translating software. That is what we call 'machine translation.' But just as machines do not replace human doctors, they are not likely to replace human translators either. Doctors can perform more and better operations with the help of high tech equipment now available.

Likewise, future translators will be able to work on more text of various genres at a higher speed, and get paid more for their higher-quality service. As recently as in the 1990s, translators had to visit libraries to get relevant information for their translation tasks. Now, almost all the necessary information is at their finger tips because it is only a few clicks away.

Corpus archives on the internet can help translators find the most natural and phrasal wording for their renditions. By now you may have realized a successful translator should also be good at using computer software, such as word processors and other research tools available on the internet.

Currently, professional translators are trained mostly at graduate-level schools. Among them are the Graduate School of Interpretation and Translation at Hankook University of Foreign Studies and a similarly named graduate schools at many other universities. The list of schools teaching translation is getting longer. Furthermore, translation education is increasingly being done at an undergraduate level. Undergraduate translation majors are offered at the Hankook University of Foreign Studies, Kyong-Hee University and Geumgang University, to name a few. As holding conventions has become something of an 'industry', the demand for translators and interpreters will continue to increase.

The demand for translators is not only from directly-related sectors, but from more indirectly- related areas. Among them is language learning, whether foreign or native. Translation is a bi-lingual process involving relevant background knowledge and sometimes non-verbal language. Students sometimes get to know more about the exact meanings of the vocabulary of their native language during the process of translating source text. Translators have a better chance of becoming a good language teacher equipped with such a knowledge base.

The surging demand for translators also means a growing market for translation teachers. Unlike those who received degrees in pure linguistics related majors, holders of degrees in translation, whether masters or doctoral, do not seem to have much difficulty finding jobs at schools. At least at the time of writing this, holders of doctoral degrees are in short supply compared to the demand from institutions of higher education. Considering recent changes in government-administered exams, the nationwide fervor in learning foreign languages, especially English, and the basic human desire for more knowledge and more prosperity, translation as a profession or as a practice will play a big, or at least a much bigger role than before. The yardstick to measure how advanced a country is will also be determined by the number of international conventions, not merely by GDP numbers. So, there should be more translators than there are now.

Text for Translation

1 철학이란 인간과 인간이 사는 세상, 그리고 그 둘 간의 관계의 근본적 진리를 탐구하는 학문이다.
⇨ Philosophers seek to understand the basic truths about themselves, the world they live in, and the **relationships between** people **and** the parts of their world.

Academic philosophy is often divided into six major branches of study: aesthetics(the study of beauty and values), metaphysics(the nature of reality), epistemology(the study of knowledge), ethics (how we should behave and why), logic (the nature and structure of argument), and history of philosophy (ideas and arguments recorded by earlier philosophers).

2 오늘은, 윤리란 무엇이며, 현대사회에서 윤리가 왜 필요한지에 대해 알아보자.

⇨ In this topic, we will **take a close look at** what ethics is and how it is used in modern society.

Because the formal study of ethics, or right behavior, has been going on for thousands of years, it is tempting to assume it is a topic of little relevance to us these days. The truth is, ethics, also known as morality, ^{도덕성} will never be irrelevant because it is of fundamental importance to our lives.

3 다른 사람과 공존하려면, 어떤 행동이 바람직하고 올바른 것인지를 알아야 한다.

⇨ To coexist with other people comfortably, we need to **know what** kinds of behaviors are reasonable and fair.

We want to know we are treating others well, and they are treating us well-founded particularly in these days of cultural confrontation. The study ^{타당성있는} of ethics has provided consistent and well- reasons for what people ought to do. This body of reason is based on factors such as our rights, duties, and fairness; as well as, the benefits to society and quality of outcomes ^{공평} of our activities.

In ethics, there are four major fields of study. Meta-ethics involves deep analysis of the meaning of moral propositions.^(명제) Also of interest to this field are the attitudes and judgments related to such propositions. Descriptive^(기술) ethics **is based on** what moral values particular groups of people live by.^(실천하다) Normative^(규범) ethics (or moral theory) is an exploration of what is right and wrong, and how that knowledge might guide moral action. Up to this point, ethics is abstract, and unfamiliar to most of us. However, within^(=dealswith) normative ethics is a specialty,^(전문분야) called applied^(응용) ethics, which touches our lives daily. In applied ethics, knowledge gained from the study of morality is used to establish policy aimed at achieving a moral outcome in a specific situation. Following is an incomplete^(전부는 아니지만) list of subjects for which ethics has major influence in our society.

Environmental Ethics Three common reasons exist as justifications for working to save the environment. First, because non-human organisms exist, they deserve to have the ethical rights we have. Second, non-human organisms need protection because we are all parts of an interdependent whole. Third, non-human organisms need conservation because many of them are useful to the human race. The trend is to expand the use of ethical considerations from humans to the rest of the world.

Some believe this should include inanimate portions (land, water, air) - others only living things. Some have urged that future generations also be given ethical consideration. Major changes in law, economics, and ecology have followed these shifts. Specific issues for ethical guidance include the queries, "Is it acceptable to destroy and degrade Nature to allow unsustainable human consumption? Have we obligations to preserve resources for future generations?"

Journalism Ethics 언론 Though not exactly uniform, there is a lot of effort to apply ethical standards by organizations in print, 신문 broadcast, and online news media. Professional journalists are expected to provide good, factual reporting using reliable witnesses. Journalists are expected to provide information that is truthful, accurate, objective, and fairly presented.

4 언론인이 남에게 피해를 주는 실수를 했다면 그에 책임져야 한다.
⇨ Journalists can expect to **be held accountable for** damaging mistakes.

Such professionals are expected to be sensitive to conditions surrounding a story. For example, some details of a story might not be published if this would cause harm to innocents. 무고한 사람 Certainly, journalists are expected to avoid use of discriminatory references, and to presume the 추정하다 innocence of people currently on trial. 무죄 재판중인 The International Federation of Journalists guides ethics abroad, whereas the Society of Professional Journalists is one major organization that does so in the USA.

Legal Ethics 법조 In the United States, each state or territory sets code 법전 a of professional conduct, often modeled on the guidelines of the American Bar Association. 변호사 Among the issues of interest are the

relationship between lawyer and client, a lawyer's duties as advocate, dealings with those who are not clients, behavior in law firms, public service, advertising legal services, and maintaining professional integrity.^{정직성} Many US law schools now require at least one course on legal ethics or professional responsibility.

Medical Ethics Generally, medical practitioners^{개업의} are expected to provide at least six major values to patients undergoing medical research or treatment. The patient should be able to accept or refuse treatment.

5 의사는 항상 환자의 이익을 최우선시해야 한다.
⇨ The practitioner should always act **in the best interest of** the patient (no secret conflicts of interest).

The actions of the practitioner should never make things worse. Scarce medicines and treatments should be distributed fairly. The patient should always be allowed basic dignity. All actions should be explained truthfully and honestly. An example of a formal result of medical ethics is the Declaration of Helsinki, which is considered the authority on applied ethics for human research.

Military Ethics

6 군대의 목적은 모든 구성원이 군의 가치나 규범에 따라 행동하게끔 하는 것이다.
⇨ The goal within the military body is to **have** all members **behave**

consistent with military values and standards. Military ethics was applied to create the Geneva Conventions, which guide treatment of victims during warfare.

Some specific issues include such as, "What is the justification for the use of war?", "How should abuse issues related to race, gender, sexual orientation and age, be handled?", and "What level of political influence should be allowed those in the military?"

Religious Ethics As well as their core beliefs, most religions also have ethical components in their teachings, often influenced by supernatural or guidance. Let's examine how some of these major religions compare.

For Buddhist laymen, the ethical foundation is the Pancasila (no killing, stealing, lying, sexual misconduct, or use of intoxicants). The Middle Way provides more practical help for moral problems. The Noble Eightfold Path declares, in particular, a doctrine of non-violence to all creatures, and implies an intimate involvement with them. The Mangala Sutra calls for the positive qualities of reverence, humility, contentment, gratitude, patience, and generosity, among others. Then there are the immeasurables, the four attitudes of loving-kindness, compassion, sympathetic joy, and calmness, that Buddhists are expected to exhibit. By meditating, chanting, and practicing selflessness, Buddhists are expected to gradually enhance their best qualities and diminish their worst.

The Christian Ethic is based on the idea of <u>Divine Grace</u>.^{신의 은총} This can transform a life and enable a person to choose and behave righteously.

7 신의 가호와 함께 기독교인들은 생각과 행동을 도덕적으로 해야 한다.

⇨ With divine assistance, Christians **are expected to** become increasingly virtuous^{도덕적} in thought and deed.

Specific guidance is given in the Old Testament: the Ten Commandments, some of the Psalms^{찬송가} and moral tales from among the historical accounts. Christians are expected to show personal integrity, avoid hypocrisy,^{위선} be honest, loyal, and merciful, forgive others their faults, reject materialism,^{물질만능주의} and teach others by example of personal joy, happiness, and Godly devotion. Jewish Ethics is said to be very similar, with one notable exception. As well as the previous, Christians are urged to love their enemies and turn the other cheek.

Expressions Review

1 relationship between ⋯ and ⋯

2 take a look at something

3 know what + noun + verb

4 hold somebody accountable for something

5 in the best interest of somebody [something]

6 have + object + root verb

7 be expected to do something

8 as well as + nouns

9 be based on something

10 consistent with something

Model Dialogue

Amy: How do ethics differ from manners?

James: Ethics has a broader concept than manners. Manners are based on ethics of a local community. As a member of your community you are expected to follow the local manners.

Amy: Why do we need ethics and manners in the first place?

James: Because it serves our common interest. It is in our best interest to maintain a standard of ethisc. It is not just a formality.

Amy: How do greetings such as 'Good morning' and 'Good bye' serve our interest, for example?

James: By saying those greetings, we can more easily communicate with others in a friendlier atmosphere. That's why in elementary schools teachers have their students bow before the class begins.

Amy: Taking a closer look at ethics, I now know that it is deeply related to reducing unnecessary frictions in our daily lives.

Talking Practice

Now, the class divides into two groups. The two groups of students sit in line facing each other. Each pair of students will talk about the topic using the expressions for 5 minutes. After each talking session is finished, students will move anticlockwise to talk to a new partner for another 5 minutes. Talking Practice ends when students meet their first partner again.

Review Test

▶ Following is part of the main text. Fill the blanks to complete the text (1 point for each blank).

The oldest recognizable remains of Life (probably ancient bacteria) have been dated to roughly 1. _____ ago. More importantly, fossils of many larger forms of Life (sea animals, plants, 2. _____ and other animals clearly not living today) have been dated at ages from hundreds of millions, to tens of millions, of years or less.***

The point is that the planet existed long before any single-celled life that we know of, and that single cells existed long before larger life forms, including 3. ___. This means that, if the scientific dating is correct, then the first part of the Bible cannot be considered an exact statement of historical fact. As some have said, that part of the Bible might best be considered a creation 4. ___ recorded by the ancestors of Christians to preserve important moral lessons for later 5. _____.***

▶ Translate the following sentences as they appear in the main text (3 points each).

1 지표면에서 발견된 암석 중 가장 오래된 것은 과학적 방법으로 추정 했을 때 약 38억년 전에 생성된 것이다.

2 우리가 만일 신앙심이 돈독하고 상당한 지적 수준을 갖춘 기독교인이 라면 이런 것들을 어떻게 설명해야 할 것인가?

3 기독교 신자들은 이 세상과 모든 생물은 하느님이 직접 만들었다고 믿는다.

4 그렇다 하더라도, 과학자들이 이러한 기술을 신봉하는 데에는 네 가 지 이유가 있다.

5 이것은 사실이 아니다.

Chapter 6 Translation as Creation

Words Speak Louder than Acts

'Be faithful to the original to the letter.' Many novice translators, or even veteran self-made translators, believe that word-for-word faithfulness is the essential hard and fast rule in translation. If it is the #1 rule in the job of translation, then the task can basically be done by existing computer software. In my other book titled, 'Translation and Subtitling (2008)', I wrote, 'translation is an informational engineering by which translators 'engineer' the linguistic and cultural message in the source text within an acceptable range and express it in the target language.' Even though there is some reservation, we need to view translation as an intellectual activity similar to creation. What is important is the content; the body inside is significant, not the clothes the body wears. It is totally up to the translator in charge how to express the contents. Unless the content is drastically altered, vocabulary or wording does not matter much. Sometimes content itself could undergo some changes whenever deemed necessary by the translator. That is where creation comes in.

Creation in translation is justified because speech calls for action. The branch of study on that specific field is 'Speech Act'. According to Speech Act, every utterance or text has its own purpose. But for some, let us say diplomatic reasons, the purpose, or the intent, is disguised under the mask of verbal or non verbal signs. If the translator thinks of his job as taking the intent from the source text, he could use a totally different set of vocabulary than the original and make the text longer, shorter. That is what amounts to 'creation.'

How much creation is accepted varies depending on the genre. Conventionally, subtitlers enjoy the widest range of creational leeway while translators of technical text, such as legal documents and user manuals, do not. More leeway in creation often translates into more responsibility for the job. In classrooms dealing with low-level text, students are encouraged to stick to the form and contents of the source text, while in classrooms teaching high-level students, teachers demand that their students get as far away as possible from the original, whether in form or in content. In subtitling classes, students are more often asked to speak their own language than in technical translations classes where they are much less so.

When you think just a little about what creation means, you will quickly realize creation is not much different from translation. We do not create things out of nothing. We create some things based on the interpretation of what we have experienced and learned. When we translate, we interpret the message the author tries to deliver and express it our own way. Don't you think some basic similarities exist between creation and translation?

That is the reason why many a great writers were and are also great translators. They get inspirations for their own work while translating others' writings. Inversely, they produce superior translations because they are better than their writing-only counterparts at 'getting into the heads' of the original authors.

Now that you realize every translation is a creation, you may also understand that there are no two identical translations for one original. If you give ten students a task of translating just one sentence, they will give you back the same number of different translations. And a thousand students will give you a thousand different translations. Why not ten thousands and even a million? Why do they each give you different versions when they have been given the same source text? Because each of them interprets the source text from her own way and '*creat*es' her own story.

Text for Translation

1 지구온난화란, 지표면 공기나 바다의 평균기온이 최근 수십 년 동안 상승했고 앞으로도 계속되리라 예상되는 현상이다.

⇨ Global warming is the **increase in** the average temperature of the Earth's near-surface air and oceans in recent decades and its projected continuation.

Global average air temperature near the Earth's surface rose 0.74 ± 0.18

℃ during the past century. The Intergovernmental Panel on Climate 〔위원회〕
Change (IPCC) concludes, "most of the observed increase in globally
averaged temperatures since the mid-20th century is very likely due to the
observed increase in anthropogenic(인간이 만든)_greenhouse gas
concentrations," which warms the surface and lower atmosphere by 〔대기〕
increasing the greenhouse effect. 〔농도〕

2 일조량의 변화나 화산폭발 등의 자연현상이 산업시대 이전부터 1950
년 까지 약간의 온난 효과를 가져온 것으로 보이나 그 이후로는 냉각
효과도 약간 있었던 것으로 보인다.

⇨ Natural phenomena such as solar variation combined with volcanoes
have probably **had** a small warming **effect** from pre-industrial times
to 1950, but a small cooling effect since 1950.

These basic conclusions have been endorsed by at least 30 scientific 〔지지되다〕
societies and academies of science, including all the national academies 〔학회〕
of science of the major industrialized countries. The American Association
of Petroleum Geologists_is the only scientific society that rejects these
conclusions, and a few individual scientists disagree with parts of them.
Climate models referenced by the IPCC, project that global surface 〔인용하다〕
temperatures are likely to increase by 1.1 to 6.4 ℃ between 1990 and
2100. The range of values reflects the use of different assumptions of
future greenhouse gas emissions and results of models with **differences**
in climate sensitivity. Although most studies focus on the period up to
2100, warming and sea level rise are expected to continue for more than

¹⁰⁰⁰년
a millennium even if greenhouse gas levels stabilize. ^{안정되다}

3 이것은 해양의 엄청난 열 수용능력과 매우 느린 변화 때문이다.
⇨ This **reflects** the large heat capacity, and slow change, of the oceans.

An increase in global temperatures can **in turn** cause other changes, including sea level rise, and changes in the amount and pattern of precipitation_resulting in floods and drought. There may also be changes in the frequency and intensity of extreme weather_events, though it is difficult to connect specific events to global warming.

4 다른 효과로는, 농작물 생산량 변화, 빙하의 퇴각, 멸종, 질병의 종류 증가 등을 들 수 있다.
⇨ Other effects may include **changes in** agricultural yields, glacier retreat, species extinctions,_and increases in the ranges of disease vectors(매개체).

5 아직 과학적으로 규명이 안된 것으로는, 미래의 기후 변화의 정확한 폭과 지역에 따른 편차다.
⇨ Remaining scientific uncertainties_include the exact degree of climate change expected in the future, and how changes will vary **from region to region** around the globe.

There is ongoing political and public debate regarding what, if any, action should be taken to reduce or reverse future warming or to adapt to its expected consequences.

6 대부분의 국가는 온실가스 배출을 규제를 목적으로 하는 교토의정서
에 서명하고 비준했다.
⇨ Most national governments have signed and ratified the Kyoto
Protocol **aimed at** combating greenhouse gas emissions.

The term "global warming" is a specific example of the broader term
climate change, which can also refer to global cooling. In common usage,
the term refers to recent warming and implies a human influence. The
United Nations Framework Convention on Climate Change (UNFCCC)
uses the term "climate change" for human-caused change and "climate
variability" for other changes. The term "climate change" is sometimes
used when focusing on human-induced changes.

7 일부 경제전문가들은 전세계 기후 변화로 인한 경제적 총손실을 추정
해왔다.
⇨ Some economists have tried to estimate the aggregate net economic
costs of **damages from** climate change across the globe.

Such estimates have so far failed to reach conclusive ; in a survey of
100 estimates, the values ran from US $10 per ton of carbon (tC) or US
$3 per ton of carbon dioxide, up to US $350/tC or US $95 per ton of
carbon dioxide, with a of US $43 per ton of carbon or US $12 per ton
of carbon dioxide. One widely publicized report on potential economic
impact is the Stern Review.

8 이상기후로 인해 전세계 GDP가 1%까지 떨어질 것으로 예상하고 있다.

⇨ It suggests that extreme weather might reduce global gross domestic product (GDP) by up to 1% **in a worst-case scenario**.

Global per capita consumption could fall 20%. The report's methodology, advocacy, and conclusions have been criticized by many economists, while others have supported the general attempt to quantify economic risk, even if not the specific numbers.

In a summary of economic cost associated with climate change, the United Nations Environment Program emphasizes the risks to insurers, reinsurers, and banks of increasingly and costly weather events. Other economic systems likely to face difficulties related to climate change include agriculture and transport.

9 선진국보다 개도국에서 그 경제적 피해가 더 클 것이다.
⇨ Developing countries, rather than the developed world, are **at** greatest economic **risk.**

Expressions Review

1 increase in ⋯

2 have effect on ⋯

3 differences in⋯

4 reflect

5 in turn

6 from region to region

7 aimed at ⋯

8 damages from⋯

9 worst-case scenario

10 at risk

Model Dialogue

Amy: Every time there is any environment-related news, I keep hearing about global warming. What's that about?

James: Global warming is a constant increase in the temperatures of the earth surface. And it has an enormous effect on how we live on Earth.

Amy: What's the difference in temperature over time so far?

James: It depends on the region. But, generally speaking, a little less than one degree Celsius, I guess. But the international community in general suffers a lot from damages due to global warming.

Amy: Planet Earth is never at peace. It's always at risk. Anyway, what is a worst-case scenario for extreme global warming? Are we all going to become extinct just like mammoths of the Ice Age?

James: Global warming warms the earth and in turn, melts the ice on the North and South poles, which elevate the sea level, thus flooding many parts of the world. Reducing carbon dioxide is part of the effort aimed at fighting global warming.

Talking Practice

Now, the class divides into two groups. The two groups of students sit in line facing each other. Each pair of students will talk about the topic using the expressions for 5 minutes. After each talking session is finished, students will move anticlockwise to talk to a new partner for another 5 minutes. Talking Practice ends when students meet their first partner again.

Review Test

▶ Following is part of the main text. Fill the blanks to complete the text (1 point for each blank).

These basic conclusions have been endorsed by at least 1.___ scientific societies and academies of science, including all the national academies of science of the major industrialized countries. The American Association of Petroleum Geologists_is the only scientific society that rejects these conclusions, and a few individual scientists disagree with parts of them. Climate models referenced by the IPCC, project that global surface temperatures are likely to increase by 2.____ to 3.____ ℃ between 4._____ and 2100. The range of values reflects the use of different assumptions of future greenhouse gas emissions and results of models with differences in climate sensitivity. Although most studies focus on the period up to 5._____, warming and sea level rise are expected to continue for more than a millennium even if greenhouse gas levels stabilize.***

▶ Translate the following Korean sentences into English (3 points each).

1 지구온난화란, 지표면 공기나 바다의 평균기온이 최근 수십 년 동안 상승했고 앞으로도 계속되리라 예상되는 현상이다

2 이것은 해양의 엄청난 열 수용능력과 매우 느린 변화 때문이다

3 대부분의 국가는 온실가스 배출을 규제를 목적으로 하는 교토 의정서에 서명하고 비준했다.

4 일부 경제전문가들은 전세계 기후 변화로 인한 경제적 총 손실을 추정해왔다

5 선진국보다 개도국에서 그 경제적 피해가 더 클 것이다.

Chapter 7   Translation as a Different Perspective

Dictionary or Different Views

What would you choose if you were allowed only one tool for a translation task? Nine times out of ten, the answer would be a dictionary. If your answer is the same, it is either because your vocabulary is too small or because you do not know the most important but widely unknown secret in translation: having a different perspective. There are more than a thousand ways to depict an elephant. You can use technical terms such as *pachyderm* or everyday descriptive words like, *thick skin*. By having a different perspective, or looking at an object from a different angle, you can choose vocabulary that you feel more comfortable with so that you do not need to use a dictionary as often as you might expect.

Translation does not mean wrestling with a thick and worn-out dictionary or searching for items from a long list of definitions on some dictionary software. Translation is more like seeing rather than writing. Translation is a race against time, but it does not mean that you have to get right into the actual translating as soon as you are confronted with the first sentence of the source text. Good translators invest more time in getting the overall picture the author is trying to draw. Only then do they decide from what angle to depict the picture. The translator's angle might not necessarily match that of the author. Chances are that the more different the translator's angle from the author's is, the better the translation will become.

But why does a different angle sometimes guarantee a better-quality translation? It is because the translator is from a different culture than the author's. First and foremost, culture is a set of perspectives. In one culture, respect for people varies with how rich they are while in another it depends on their job. In one culture, raising a middle finger is an act of insult while it is not in another. Likewise, specific words in one language might mean something completely different in another language. Translation bridges two languages, and thus, two cultures. To take a different point of view, you must first be good at *visualizing*.

Visualization simplifies the message in the source text so that you can depict the visual image with the words you choose, with an order you choose, and more importantly, at a length you choose. Once the translator has visualized the text, it is not the words that matter, but the overall message of the original. To visualize the message, you have to read the entire source text before proceeding. Time spent in the visualization process will be compensated tenfold later and will prove to be time-saving for the entire task.

Simply following the words in the source text seems to be the safest route to take for many novice translators when actually it is the most risky route to lousy, long, and overdue translations. Translating word-for-word is never a translation because it does not show a trace of creative effort on the translator's part. Translators should first take control of the source text, not be controlled by it. That is especially true for verbal translation, or interpretation. The speed of visualization decides the speed of your translating job, and thus, your reputation as a translator in this profession. Subtitlers, on the other hand, do not need to visualize as much because their text comes with visual images.

Text for Translation

1 가치론이란, 가치의 본질과 종류를 다루는 철학의 한 분과이다.

⇨ is the branch of philosophy dealing with the nature and kinds of value.

This knowledge of values is at the root of inquiries into morality, aesthetics, religion, and metaphysics. Here, we will explore the branch of philosophy called aesthetics, and see how knowledge of values is important to it.

Since the word 'aesthetics' is used to mean various things, we will choose a specific definition. Here, aesthetics means the philosophical investigation of the meaning of Beauty, how we recognize Beauty and why.

2 특히, 미학의 목적은 아름다움의 심오한 본질을 이해하는 것이다.

⇨ **In particular**, aesthetics is the attempt to understand the deeper nature of Beauty.

For example, a person, building, fragrance, song, or mathematical proof, each could be interpreted as beautiful. It is in aesthetics, that questions like, "How is it possible that such different things can be beautiful?" or "What qualities do they possess that make them all seem beautiful?" We also need to distinguish aesthetics, from tastes. At first, the tastes of people vary by class, culture, and education. After social negotiation and education, good taste can be learned.

Recognition and appreciation of Beauty, is a powerful force for good in our lives. We can apply a good sense of aesthetics and refined good taste when we work with art and other forms of culture. These are products of humankind. We may also apply aesthetics to the perception of Truth as Beauty: as in mathematics, analytic philosophy, and physics, and to the appreciation of Nature - both human beauty and to regions unaltered by people. When we share appreciation for Beauty, we have more common ground for communication. The sense of value for Beauty also gives us the means to take pleasure, relaxation, and refreshment from our surroundings. This improves our quality of life.

The question of whether an aesthetic common to all people exists is a matter of debate. It is safe to claim there are aesthetic properties in some naturally occurring phenomena that appeal to all human beings on some basic level. Landscape vistas,^(풍경) the unspoiled night sky, and the human body are aesthetically pleasing. They also have an emotional effect on the viewer, and are considered in their appeal. However they **come about**, our decisions about how to value Beauty influence our daily lives.

We use our aesthetics when we work with art and music. In modern times, expressions of art and music have expanded into entirely new media. Film, television and online made possible by the development of new technology, have also required new rules of aesthetics. These in turn affect those practical areas that draw great influence from arts, such as marketing, promotion, and design of all kinds of marketable products.

3 환경운동의 상당 부분은 자연의 미학과 관련이 있다.
⇨ A substantial part of the environmental movement **is concerned with** the aesthetics of nature.

For many people, sight of an undisturbed natural vista brings a unique form of joy. When working with land, aesthetic choices have to be made. Ideally, a mountain range or desert landscape under consideration would be conserved either as it is, or be restored to its original state. However, if that land is a park site meant to accommodate tourists, recreational excursions, or wildlife rehabilitation, some development must occur. Aesthetically sensitive development requires judgments about many things. These might include the number and types of roads, buildings, and other infrastructure; the color, shape, and type of materials used to construct them; and the decisions on where to place them within any given site. Roads are the primary means of access for people, vehicles and goods, but their effect on the landscape and on the local ecosystem means that their construction is carefully thought out. After all, the main reason people go to nature sites is to enjoy unspoiled views and see in its native habitat. Similarly, buildings that contain rest rooms, information centers, restaurants, or accommodation usually reflect the surrounding landscape: wood and stone that match the surrounding forest, or stones **similar in color to** the desert sand surrounding the building.

Aesthetics can also play a large part in deciding how economic development advances. California, (USA), is developing projects that will substantially increase renewable energy generation. The Mojave Desert has sunny weather most of each year and is ideal for generating solar energy.

4 그러나 태양발전소를 짓는데 안성맞춤인 부지는 사막 산맥의 보호구역에 있는 빼어난 경관지구 안에 있다.

⇨ However, the area best **suited for** solar power plants are located within magnificent landscapes of protected desert mountain ranges.

As a result, new laws have been to preserve the low, flat areas in these vistas because many people prefer an unspoiled vista of extinct volcanoes and sand dunes overgrown with desert scrub (bushes and shrubs). Similarly, off the northeast coast of America in the region known as New England, wind blows strong and long for most of the year. Some time ago, a project was started to put large wind turbines well off that shore.

No doubt, local officials felt that they were doing a very good thing. There would have been no carbon emissions or fossil fuel consumption, the energy would have been sustainable, and the turbine noise unable to bother any residents.

5 그럼에도 불구하고, 아주 많은 사람들이 풍력발전기의 모습에 불쾌해 하는 바람에 그 계획은 중단되고 말았다.

⇨ **Even so**, a sufficiently large number of people were offended by the sight of wind turbines offshore that the project was stopped.

Architecture is another area of activity where aesthetics is keenly important. Since most architecture is public, there must be an attempt early in each project to come to an aesthetic consensus among the project people and the local community that will have to live with the new structure. Every structure is the result of large numbers of aesthetic choices. These might include design, materials, the structure itself and how it will interact with the community. Excellent projects, such as the Sydney Opera House, often go on to become international icons. Modern bridges are also often boldly beautiful.

In visual design, many aesthetic preferences inform what is made and presented to consumers. How a website is designed is **of importance** because the aesthetics of a site is directly connected to how well it performs. With companies and organizations moving increasing amounts of services and information onto the World Wide Web, there is a lot at stake in how well a web page attracts and keeps users. This is especially relevant for companies that sell products or services over the Internet. The aesthetics of a page are judged the instant it loads. If the page is unappealing, or if the desired information is not easily found, users go elsewhere or part with their money reluctantly.

Another area where aesthetics is essential in marketing is the food service industry. We are all keenly to textural, visual, odor, and taste qualities of food. It is the job of chefs, servers, and food product companies to process and present foods that are aesthetically pleasing. Restaurant aesthetics must include the architecture and interior design, wait staff apparel, and menu items as well. Food sold in markets must not only taste good, but must also draw the attention of shoppers. For this reason, companies spend a lot on both the food products and their packaging.

This treatment is not nearly complete, but it should be clear how important aesthetic decisions are, even in our modern lives.

6 우리는 매력적인 사람이나 물건을 보면 감정적으로 강하게 반응한다.
⇨ We have strong emotional **responses to** attractive people and attractive things.

Because this response has commercial implications, aesthetics will always exert a strong influence over what we purchase. We can use aesthetics to improve our quality of life by surrounding ourselves with objects and conditions that are beautiful.

7 우리는 또한 공원, 야생동물 보호구역 등 주변의 풍경이 우리 내면 깊숙이 감춰진 자연미에 대한 기준과 일치하는지를 확인하는 노력을 기울일 수 있다.

⇨ We can also **make efforts to** see the development around us, including parks and wildlife areas, **are consistent with** our deeply held values about the beauty of Nature.

Expressions Review

1 in particular

2 be concerned with ⋯

3 be suited for ⋯

4 Even so

5 respond to ⋯

6 make efforts to + verb

7 be consistent with ⋯

8 come about

9 similar to ⋯

Model Dialogue

Amy: Aesthetics? What's that about? In particular, what does it deal with, in particular?

James: Aesthetics is concerned with the question of 'what is beautiful?' But don't simply think the study of aesthetics is only suited for women.

Amy: When did the study come about?

James: It began as a part of philosophy. Ancient thinkers wanted to find out why people respond to something beautiful and what beautiful things have in common.

Amy: I see. People these days are making every effort to make things beautiful. I think it is consistent with human nature to make things more beautiful.

James: Right. The aesthetical aspect of product design is becoming more important; so aesthetics is not only about emotions, but also about economics.

Amy: That's why some people say economics is pretty similar to human psychology.

Talking Practice

Now, the class divides into two groups. The two groups of students sit in line facing each other. Each pair of students will talk about the topic using the expressions for 5 minutes. After each talking session is finished, students will move anticlockwise to talk to a new partner for another 5 minutes. Talking Practice ends when students meet their first partner again.

Review Test

▶ Following is part of the main text. Fill the blanks to complete the text (1 point for each blank).

Recognition and appreciation of Beauty, is a powerful force for 1._____ in our lives. We can apply a good sense of aesthetics and refined good taste when we work with art and other forms of 2. _____. These are products of humankind. We may also apply aesthetics to the perception of Truth as Beauty: as in mathematics, analytic philosophy, and physics, and to the appreciation of Nature - both human beauty and to regions unaltered by people. When we share appreciation for Beauty, we have more common ground for 3. _____. The sense of value for Beauty also gives us the 4._____ to take pleasure, relaxation, and refreshment from our surroundings. This improves our 5._____.

▶ Translate the following Korean sentences into English (3 points each).

1 가치론이란, 가치의 본질과 종류를 다루는 철학의 한 분과이다.

2 특히, 미학의 목적은 아름다움의 심오한 본질을 이해하는 것이다.

3 환경운동의 상당 부분은 자연의 미학과 관련이 있다.

4 그러나 태양발전소를 짓는데 안성맞춤인 부지는 사막 산맥의 보호구역에 있는 빼어난 경관지구 안에 있다.

5 그럼에도 불구하고, 아주 많은 사람들이 풍력발전기의 모습에 불쾌해하는 바람에 그 계획은 중단되고 말았다.

Chapter 8

Translation as Techniques

Change whatever you want

Translation as an art requires an infinite number of techniques to maximize its naturalness and conciseness for the target reader. Fortunately this large set of translation techniques can be categorized into six. The first three are one family while the other three are another. Generalization, specification, and substitution are grouped by semantic field. Localization, foreignization, and neutralization are classified by cultural background.

Generalization There are times when translators have a hard time finding appropriate target text wording for specific, original words and phrases. Translators in this situation might prefer to give up on finding the exact counterpart in the target language. Instead, the translator should try to find more general wording which has the properties that are most important to the meaning of the original part in question.

Specification If language A expresses an idea more generally than language B, the translator who works from A to B must specify the source text meaning for his target reader. For example, the English word, 'brother' does not specify whether the brother is younger or older. When you translate to Korean, you have to make it clear whether the brother is *hyung* (elder brother) or *donsaeng* (younger).

Substitution If language A expresses an idea which is new to the target reader, the translator may choose a different idea which he thinks is easier for the target reader to understand. For example, the English phrase 'the size of the State of Rhode Island' could be substituted by 'the size of Hong Kong'. If the target reader could more easily guess the size of Hong Kong rather than that of the State of Rhode Island, make use of substitution.

Localization Translation is often called 'localization' because for some people translating is simply to localize the source text messages for local readers. Localization is more commonly used in countries where people do not have much knowledge about the source language and/or much contact with the source culture. For example, 'pie in the sky' may be translated into Korean meaning 'rice cake in a picture' according to localization technique. 'Pie' becomes 'rice cake' in the translation. But as globalization is spreading far and wide, the localization technique is now not as common as in the past.

Foreignization As opposed to localization, foreignizing technique brings the target reader closer to the author. Translation scholars who support foreignization say the main purpose of translation is to expose target readers to things new and exotic and to serve as a culture bridge. The foreignization technique is more often observed when translators work from a major language into a minor one, for example, from English into

Korean.

Neutralization If the translator thinks neither localization nor foreignization is an appropriate technique to apply, he could resort to the third technique: neutralization. Not happy with neither 'pie' nor 'rice cake', you could 'neutralize' by choosing 'food'.

These techniques may be applied separately or, more often, collectively. Using translation techniques usually comes with a price tag: distorting the message in the original. The translator as a decision maker had to decide which technique to use and what message to give up for maximizing the efficiency and effectiveness of communication.

Text for Translation

1 인간이 지구상에 존재하기 시작한 이래로, 자연재해는 예측불허와 정기적인 영향력을 통해 인간사에 크나큰 영향을 미쳐왔다.
⇨ For **so long as** there have been people, natural disasters have caused unpredictable, periodic effects that have shaped human history.

From (study of human origins) and (study of ancient climates), numerous examples have been found where earthquakes and volcanoes have destroyed entire cities or where severe droughts have brought down whole civilizations.

Very often, disasters like these affect a limited area, with casualties and damage only to the local people and their settlements. One of the most famous examples of local effects is from the eruption of Mount Vesuvius in 79 AD. Shortly after a major eruption, a cloud of hot gas and volcanic ash swept over the Roman cities of Pompeii and Herculaneum. Because the volcanic cloud (pyroclastic flow: 용암류) was around 1000 degrees C, and moved at hundreds of km/hr, it burned, and then buried all living things in those cities within minutes.

2 다른 경우 자연재해는 과거뿐 아니라 오늘날에도 오랜 시간과 넓은 지역에 엄청난 영향력을 미친다.

⇨ Other natural disasters have **had**, and still have today, wide-ranging global **consequences** across space and time.

3 고대인류학의 이론에 따르면, 10만년 전 동아프리카 지역의 대가뭄이 인간의 진화사를 크게 바꾸어 놓았다고 한다.

⇨ Paleoanthropologists have a theory that a major drought in East Africa around 100,000 years ago completely changed human evolution.

Evidence for this 'mega-drought' has been found in the geological record. Sediments from Lake Malawi in East Africa show the water level in the lake dropped about 600 meters, indicating a major, long-term shift from a tropical climate to a desert one.

4 현대유전학에서는, 현존하는 인류의 조상은 이때의 자연재해를 견뎌 낸 약 2천명의 사람들인 것으로 추정한다.

⇨ Modern genetics suggests that all humans alive today are descended from a group of around two thousand people who **managed to** survive this natural disaster.

This is the reason populations all over the world are genetically compatible and biologically similar. The offspring of this small group of survivors, the ones who had been best able to cope with these disastrous conditions, went on to the entire planet.

In modern times, there have also been major disasters that have had regional or global impacts. Two extreme examples of such large-scale disasters originated in Indonesia.

5 이들 섬은 매우 다양한 인류문화와 생물학적 종의 본거지다.
⇨ These islands **are home to** an enormous diversity of human cultures and biological species.

They also happen to sit on the Ring of Fire, the region surrounding the Pacific Ocean where most of the world's earthquakes and volcanic activity occurs.

Java is Indonesia's most populous island and where the capital city, Jakarta, is located. East of Java is another island, Sumbawa, where a volcano called Mount Tambora stands.

6 1815년, 지진기록 이후 초대형 화산폭발이 그 곳에서 발생했다.
⇨ In 1815, **the largest** volcanic eruption **ever** recorded took place there.

Pyroclastic flows affected villages near the base of the volcano, and drifting volcanic ash smothered crops over a large area, including nearby islands. The eruption is thought to have **resulted in** more than 70,000 deaths, including both starvation from the disruption of agriculture, and deaths from the pyroclastic flows. This was bad, but the effects of this eruption would continue over a much greater space and time.

The explosion that took place at Mount Tambora sprayed a tremendous amount of small particles, particularly sulfur compounds, high into the atmosphere. These particles remained suspended high in the atmosphere and had a powerful cooling effect on the global climate in 1816. Along with the particles remaining from several much smaller volcanic explosions that took place around the world in previous years, the cumulative effects resulted in what was called the 'Year without a Summer'.

Extremely unusual weather conditions occurred in the Northern Hemisphere during that year. Low temperatures persisted during what was supposed to be summer. There are **documented** cases of frozen rivers and lakes, snowfall accumulation, and frost in places where the temperature during the day should have been well above 20° Celsius. Crops that usually thrive in the summer were lost, and famine occurred in many places, including China and countries in Europe. Worldwide, there were hundreds of thousands of deaths from starvation, diseases, and other misfortunes caused by the rapid climate change. Another disaster with global consequences took place near the end of 2004. Off the western coast of the Indonesian island of Sumatra, a major 'mega-thrust' earthquake was one of the most powerful ever recorded, and triggered other earthquakes as far away as North America. The deadliest aspect of this earthquake was caused by a sudden upthrust [용기] of sea bottom along a fault [단층] 1600 Km long. This motion rapidly displaced about 30 km^3 of seawater and triggered massive tsunamis up to 15 m high that devastated coasts around the Indian Ocean. The **hardest hit** countries were Indonesia, Sri Lanka, India, and Thailand. In almost all these places, the tsunami hit without warning. People were either still in their homes or on the street, when a series of water walls up to 15 m high rushed in from the coast to as far as two kilometers inland. The surging, churning waters were also filled with debris.

7 이 엄청난 상황들이 맞물려 25만으로 추정되는 사람들이 사망했다.
⇨ This deadly combination of circumstances **proved fatal** for an estimated 250,000 people.

In addition, notable about this tragedy was the substantial media news coverage and foreign aid from developed nations despite the fact developing countries that were hit hardest. December was peak tourist season in the region and there were almost 10,000 foreigners listed among the dead and missing, most of them from Europe.

8 이 재해를 계기로 제 3세계의 자연재해에 대한 국제사회의 문제의식이 크게 높아졌다.

⇨ This caused global concern **of much greater proportion than usual** for third world natural disasters.

This increased attention also helped to gain support and funding for an early warning detection system in the Indian Ocean that should help to minimize future **casualties**.
인명피해

9 해안지역의 재난은 새삼스러운 것은 아니지만, 그 인명/재산 피해가 엄청나게 커진 것은 현대에 들어와서이다.
⇨ Though coastal damage of various kinds has occurred since there have been coasts, it is in modern times that damage to people and their homes have become catastrophic.

This is due to the settling of more people in seismically active zones (지진대) where volcanoes and earthquakes are common, and along coasts vulnerable to tsunamis and oceanic storms. Natural disasters have different consequences in different regions and societies. This shows that good government policies can mitigate their effects.
reduce

The opposite is also true, as was clearly witnessed by global observers in summer 2005 when Hurricane Katrina hit the northern Gulf Coast of the USA. Estimates were that storm damage cost about US$125 billion, and was the costliest natural disaster in the country's history. Nearly 2000 individuals perished and the lives of millions were disrupted. Though it was not a direct hit, the storm and related flooding devastated New

Orleans, one of America's most historical cities; which to this day has not fully recovered.

The natural disaster born of Hurricane Katrina was the result of three factors. First, was the storm itself, whose severe winds laid waste a large part of the Gulf Coast. Second, was wind-driven flooding and related <u>levee failures (제방 붕괴)</u> in several areas of the city.

10 허리케인의 규모와 파괴력은 엄청났으며, 제방이 붕괴되지 않았었더라도 엄청난 피해를 냈을 것이다.

⇨ The hurricane's size and strength was exceptional and **would have caused** great damage even without the failed levees.

It was the third reason —poor official reaction – that received intense public scrutiny and caused outrage. Clear errors in leadership, poor public policy decisions, and government mishandling resulted in unnecessary suffering and delays in rescue. **Adding** (설상가상으로), after the storm struck on 29 August, parts of the roadways serving the city were damaged or flooded. This prevented emergency services rapid access into the city. It was also true that large portions of the city were flooded. This meant that all emergency activities had to be done from boats, which had to be brought in from undamaged areas. Furthermore, all but one television station, most phone lines and nearly all cell phone facilities were destroyed or damaged, and thus useless for emergency communications. Not until 4 September, were conditions stabilized.

Before Hurricane Katrina hit, a largely successful evacuation still left tens of thousands of vulnerable people in New Orleans. Some had chosen not to leave their homes, but many of those remaining were people too poor to relocate. Many of these, including young children, elderly, and disabled people, were trapped in a few overcrowded relief centers. These became sites of lawlessness, filth, and enormous suffering. Though emergency management officials claimed to have stockpiles of emergency supplies nearby, delayed relief efforts left those people without food and water for several hot, stressful days.

Poor maintenance and some faulty designs resulted in at least 50 breaches of the levees that were meant to keep water out of the lower parts of New Orleans.

11 제방 붕괴의 원인조사 결과, 미 육군 공병대는 태풍에 대비해 제방에 대한 적절한 조치를 취하지 않았음이 밝혀졌다.

⇨ Investigations of those failed levees revealed the US **Army Corp of Engineers** had not **taken the steps** needed to insure the levees would provide enough protection in such a storm event.

Natural disasters sometimes display the best of human behavior, not just its faults. In 2010, a major earthquake struck Haiti. This was the second nation to break free from colonial rule, but unfortunately, since that time, foreign intervention and local corruption have **prevented it from** ever fulfilling its potential. Thus, it is no surprise the country and its capitol city, Port-Au-Prince, were very poor places and completely unable to cope with the disaster when the earthquake leveled much of the capitol.

A large amount of foreign aid was rapidly committed, but was slow in arriving to those in need. Partly, this was because of the country's location in the Caribbean Sea, but even more so, due to the countries poor infrastructure and a lack of command-and-control administration. Despite these conditions, people organized spontaneously^{자발적} within their neighborhoods to provide security, and to share vital necessities like food and water. Haitians have not been able to depend on their own government or foreign powers for assistance in the past, so individuals in Haiti have always come together in difficult times. Where there are so few national resources, people have had to depend on one another for survival.

Natural disasters will always strike unpredictably. Without a doubt, people and their settlements will continue to suffer from catastrophe in the future.

12 재난이 아무리 크더라도, 비상 인프라 또는 취약지역의 주민을 돕는 구호시설을 갖춘다면, 그로 인한 피해는 줄일 수 있다.
⇨ **No matter how extensive** the damage is, though, by developing emergency infrastructure and other resources to assist populations in vulnerable areas, the effects can be reduced.

Expressions Review

1 as long as

2 have consequences on

3 manage to + verb

4 be home to …

5 superlative + ever

6 result in …

7 prove + adjective

8 no matter how + adjective[adverb]

9 would have + past particle

10 prevent sb from doing sth

Model Dialogue

Amy: Have you ever heard about tsunamis before?

James: Of course. I will never forget about the last tsunami as long as I live. It was the largest wall of water I've ever seen.

Amy: Tell me more about it.

James: It literally swept thru the shores of Indonesia. And it had catastrophic consequences on Indonesia's tourism industry.

Amy: What happened to your family while you were there?

James: My family managed to get away from the area and came back home safely. Without the help from the local people, we would have all been killed by those enormous waves.

Amy: No matter how advanced technology becomes, it cannot prevent those natural disasters from happening without any notice.

Talking Practice

Now, the class divides into two groups. The two groups of students sit in line facing each other. Each pair of students will talk about the topic using the expressions for 5 minutes. After each talking session is finished, students will move anticlockwise to talk to a new partner for another 5 minutes. Talking Practice ends when students meet their first partner again.

Review Test

▶ Following is part of the main text. Fill the blanks to complete the text (1 point for each blank).

The opposite is also true, as was clearly witnessed by global observers in summer 1. _____ when Hurricane 2. _____ hit the northern Gulf Coast of the USA. Estimates were that storm damage cost about US$ 3. _____ billion, and was the costliest natural disaster in the country's history. Nearly 4. _____ individuals perished and the lives of millions were disrupted. Though it was not a direct hit, the storm and related flooding devastated 5. _____, one of America's most historical cities; which to this day has not fully recovered.

▶ Translate the following Korean sentences into English (3 points each).

1 인간이 지구상에 존재하기 시작한 이래로, 자연재해는 예측불허와 정기적인 영향력을 통해 인간사에 크나큰 영향을 미쳐왔다.

2 다른 경우 자연재해는 과거뿐 아니라 오늘날에도 오랜 시간과 넓은 지역에 엄청난 영향력을 미친다.

3 고대인류학의 이론에 따르면, 10만년 전 동아프리카 지역의 대가뭄이 인간의 진화사를 크게 바꾸어 놓았다고 한다.

4 현대유전학에서는, 현존하는 인류의 조상은 이때의 자연재해를 견뎌낸 약 2천명의 사람들로 추정한다.

5 이들 섬은 매우 다양한 인류문화와 생물학적 종의 본거지다.

Chapter 9 — Translation as Language Learning

Translators Try to Learn

The beauty of translation as a tool for learning foreign languages is that it requires the learner to know first what the message is he wants to express. The common sequence in teaching or learning a foreign language is from grammar, vocabulary, reading, speaking and to writing only in the foreign language. Translation is about comparison between the two languages: the foreign language and the native one. This is true whether your foreign language is at a beginner level or at an advanced level. By comparing every aspect of the two languages, you get to know more clearly about each language. Many linguists agree that learning a foreign language after acquiring one's native language is more effective and more desirable. This consensus implies that the native language is a stepping stone from which to learn foreign languages.

Translating practice helps you enhance your command of foreign languages because translating involves knowing more about the relevant knowledge. The purpose of communication, verbal or nonverbal, is to convey messages. Without things to talk about, what is the point of a simple act of talking? To master a foreign language, you have first to be curious about the people who speak the language and the culture where the language is used. Intellectual curiosity is one of the main traits required for a successful translator. A good command of both A language (your native language) and B language (a foreign language) is important but not everything.

Translation is also about creative writing. We have discussed this issue in Chapter Four. Translation is about telling a story, or communication. We have also discussed translation as storytelling in Chapter Five. Translation is about culture. We have discussed this topic in many chapters, especially in Chapter Nine which introduces translation techniques through culture. Translation is public speaking because translators work in many cases for the general public. In a nutshell, the translator is a good learner and teacher of both the foreign language and his native language.

Translation techniques are universal, which means they could be applied to any set of two languages, whether from Chinese to Japanese or from Korean to ancient Greek. The universality of translation techniques implies that by becoming a good translator of any one language, you could also more easily and quickly learn another new foreign language than those who have not had any translation education or training.

1 문명이 발생한지 얼마 되지 않아 일정한 정착 유형이 생겨나기 시작했다.

⇨ It **wasn't long after** civilization started **that** a recurring pattern of settlement began to occur.

Perhaps due to our tribal beginnings, people seemed most comfortable building in what might be called neighborhoods. Even in larger cities, people operated on smaller scales that allowed them to live and work in the same area most of the time. In these home areas, their basic needs could be met, they were familiar with their surroundings, and they knew their neighbors. In many places, this was true until roughly the end of World War II.

Then, a series of urban experiments began that redefined planning and development in horrible ways. Those were the times of poverty projects; large scale, cookie-cutter housing tracts with cul-de-sac (dead end) roads cut off from the surrounding cities; and urban business centers that became crime-ridden ghost towns after people fled to the safety of the suburbs night after night.

2 그 이후 세계 많은 곳에서는 이러한 식의 도시개발로 인해 많은 사람들이 고통을 겪었다.

⇨ Many people in various countries have since suffered **due to** similar urban design techniques.

It is now clear that these were mistakes, and a highly focused effort is already under way to do better. This movement, called "New Urban Design", has gathered and organized many of the best, tried-and-true, ideas for planning and building our towns and cities. Largely, this approach represents a new look at how and why people have always before settled into neighborhoods or villages. Some new ideas have been applied to activities that extend further than neighborhoods or cities, as well as for some modern challenges such as automotive transportation and related parking needs.

We are able to consider only some of the main points here, but let's get an overview of the levels of New Urban Design, briefly: region, neighborhoods, streets, and buildings. New Urban Design sees each city as a circle with its edges starting in the countryside, moving through a suburban area, and ending up in an urban center. Because of this, there are different rules and population densities for each of these zones. In particular, the open space and agriculture of the countryside should be preserved. Some projects such as long distance transportation, waterways, and power generation facilities require regional planning outside the city. These have different guidelines.

Second, consider some important guidelines for neighborhoods. Goals differ depending on whether the neighborhoods are in the urban, suburban, or rural zones. For example, there are different target densities for population.

3 일정 공간에 사는 사람의 숫자가 많아질수록, 돈벌이의 기회도 많아진다.

⇨ **The more** people that can comfortably live in a space, **the more** business it can support.

This makes it much easier to provide all the helpful support we need in a neighborhood: restaurants, entertainment, banks and so on. At the same time, high densities in rural areas mean development when we want preservation. Public facilities like schools and meeting places are carefully planned to reduce the need for cars. Each neighborhood is planned to include both offices and residences.

4 동시에 주택은 모든 부류의 사람들(미혼자, 기혼자, 연령, 은퇴자, 장애인, 대가족, 경제여건 등)의 다양한 욕구를 충족시켜야 한다.

⇨ At the same time, housing should **address** the needs of people of all kinds: single, married, young, retired, disabled, those of different family sizes and those of various financial conditions.

The New Urban Design movement holds strong views on streets. First, streets should not divide communities or endanger children. Within neighborhoods, traffic speeds should be slow, roads narrow, and pedestrians should **have free access to** the streets. Such streets should join communities, not separate them, because this would reduce the efficiency of emergency services, mass transit, and deliveries. Streets should have a lot of **plant and tree cover** to provide beauty and shade. There should also be arrangements for water to drain into the soil beside the streets, rather than running directly into sewers^{하수도} or flooding the area. In urban business areas, parking should be along streets and should not be plentiful. The goal is to have people utilize mass transit, rather than their cars, when they move into the urban center. Since this can challenge certain businesses, a good mass transit system must be in place and widely available to the downtown area.

Finally, the views of New Urban Design on individual buildings are reflective of other modern building trends. Of course, there are different guidelines for public and private buildings, but some goals are true for both. We should be building our structures to last: strong and durable.

5 동시에, 구조물은 쉽게 해체되고 건설자재는 재활용될 수 있도록 설계되어야 한다.

⇨ At the same time, we should design our structures **so that** they can be more easily disassembled, and **so that** most of the construction materials of which they are made, can be used again.

All new buildings should reflect the latest standards in energy and water efficiency; older buildings should be renovated so that they are not so wasteful. In particular, designs should allow use of natural light and ventilation^{환기}. Construction materials should be renewable, durable, produced with minimal use of energy and manufactured with safe chemicals.

6 가능하면, 현지에서 생산되어야 한다.

⇨ **Whenever possible**, they should be manufactured locally.

There are a lot of other ideas typical of the thinking of those in New Urban Design, and we will go over a number of them below. Let's start with mass transit. To be brief, cities will work well only when the role of individual automobiles is greatly reduced. With each car eliminated from use, the need for parking, the likelihood of accidents and theft, and the amount of air pollution and fuel inefficiency are also reduced. To accomplish this, urban areas will be designed around major mass transit corridors with other forms of mass transit between them. Both business and residential development will also be linked to these same corridors. Innovative technologies, such as individual transit pods, promise to be much more efficient, safer, and convenient than many of the mass transit methods used today.

Another new approach to management of urban areas is to make cities as self-sufficient as possible. This includes things like urban agriculture, energy production, and water and waste management. Most modern foods have a number of negative features. First, they are often grown far from where they are consumed so that transport adds a lot to their cost. Because they will be sent long distances, they are never picked when they are most ripe. We could save money and have foods that are both healthier and tastier, if they were grown and consumed locally. As much as possible, renewable energy use will be expanded to reduce demand for distant sources of energy. Conservation, water recycling, and water capture will be explored to extend existing water supplies. Local reuse of all kinds of wastes will be explored to reduce losses with emphasis placed on promoting small businesses that can provide most products and services locally. A good number of parks and places where people can go to experience nature and relax should be developed in neighborhoods and regions. A good starting point is in areas that have been badly degraded by industrial activities or pollution. These are risky places to develop, which makes them good places to restore as natural areas, with reasonable precautions. Wetlands and other water features, in particular, are always welcome additions to a community – if they attract wildlife, even better. In other cases, cities may already have mountain, valley, or other views that are covered, or threatened with development.

7 이런 경관을 일반인들이 이용하게끔 하는 것은 지역사회에 매우 긍정적인 영향을 준다.
⇨ Keeping such scenery **accessible to** the public has a powerful positive effect on the community.

The same is true of waterside areas. When these are left available for use by the public along their edges, citizens are more likely to embrace development.

City blocks need to be given a great deal of thought as well. Where there is a lot of foot traffic, blocks should be small, with lots of openings through the bases of buildings. There should be a good mix of small businesses on the ground level **with easy access** to **pedestrians**, cyclists and those using mass transit. Sidewalks in these regions need to be very wide to support not only **passersby** but also to safely accommodate small vendors.

Air quality should be kept as high as possible by discouraging car use nearby. At night, streetlights should be attractive and just bright enough to encourage evening activities. There are times when high land prices or little available space means that large, tall buildings are the best to build. One such building may serve many more purposes than a smaller one. Such a large building should always be located near mass transit to ease the need for parking and to reduce traffic in its area. On the other hand, commercial structures only a few stories high are often useful both downtown and in suburban neighborhoods. They usually serve as both dwelling and workspace at the same time. Usually the first floor is used for business while the upper parts are used for residences. In both cases, whether we use mass transit to go to work, or avoid travel altogether by living at our workplace, at least some people may eliminate the need for a private car.

Last are a few comments about the planning process. Planning and development will take a bit longer, but will go much more smoothly, if community members are included in the planning process. In this way, city planners can detect points of strong opposition and try to educate the public to the real need, or accommodate their desires, and change the plan to a more acceptable one.

8 도시계획은 세금으로 이루어지므로, 해당지역 주민들의 여론을 수렴해야 하는 것은 어쩌면 당연한 일이다.

⇨ Urban planning is mostly done with public money, **so** it is not unreasonable to gather and consider the viewpoints of the people most affected.

It is best for each community, to determine an organization that has the authority to speak for the community and then work with them. The information can be spread using mass media, or more directly through meetings. It is time consuming, but not more time consuming than cancelling a large project before it is finished.

At its heart, New Urban Design contains a series of guidelines that list the most important things a good, modern, green city ought to incorporate.

9 이러한 지침은 상가와 주택지역을 적절히 혼합하는 것을 매우 중요하게 다룬다.

⇨ These guidelines **give** a lot of **emphasis to** mixing neighborhoods so that they contain both commercial and residential buildings.

In such areas, many people can both live and work within the same community. There is a lot of emphasis on reducing the need for cars and making streets safer for kids and other pedestrians. There is a lot of emphasis on sustainable building, building to last and designing for energy efficiency.

There is emphasis on the positive roles played by parks, natural areas and other centers of beauty within the settled area. Taken altogether, it's as if common sense has been combined with a compassion for people and a strong sense of environmental responsibility.

10 과거에 비해 오늘날의 도시계획은 인간복지를 매우 중요시하는 추세다.

⇨ **Compared with** urban design techniques of the past, this movement appears genuinely **concerned with** the welfare of the humans who will reside in these reformed areas.

Expressions Review

1 have access to somewhere

2 S + V so that S + V

3 whenever possible

4 S + V, so S + V

5 give emphasis to something

6 compared with something

7 concerned with something

8 address = deal with, cope with

9 due to something

10 the more ···, the more

Model Dialogue

Amy: James, which do you prefer to live in: the city or the rural countryside?

James: Absolutely in the city.

Amy: Why? I like the rural countryside much better.

James: Cities provide much easier access to amenities such as shopping malls, hospitals... you name it. According to a recent survey, the closer you live to a hospital, the longer you'll live. You can run to the hospital whenever you want.

Amy: Compared with the city, the countryside has fewer amenities, but you can still enjoy a more peaceful and less stressful life than in the rural countryside.

James: So those concerned with city planning try to make urban environments more eco-friendly than ever before. I know cities have many problems to be addressed, such as crime and pollution due to the high population density.

Amy: That's the reason why the current president emphasizes moving the capital city down south than his predecessors.

Talking Practice

Now, the class divides into two groups. The two groups of students sit in line facing each other. Each pair of students will talk about the topic using the expressions for 5 minutes. After each talking session is finished, students will move anticlockwise to talk to a new partner for another 5 minutes. Talking Practice ends when students meet their first partner again.

Review Test

▶ Following is part of the main text. Fill the blanks to complete the text (1 point for each blank).

The opposite is also true, as was clearly witnessed by global observers in summer 1. _____ when Hurricane 2. _____ hit the northern Gulf Coast of the USA. Estimates were that storm damage cost about US$ 3. _____ billion, and was the costliest natural disaster in the country's history. Nearly 4. _____ individuals perished and the lives of millions were disrupted. Though it was not a direct hit, the storm and related flooding devastated 5. _____, one of America's most historical cities; which to this day has not fully recovered.

▶ Translate into English as they appear in the main text. (3 points each)

1 인간이 지구상에 존재하기 시작한 이래로, 자연재해는 예측불허와 정기적인 영향력을 통해 인간사에 크나큰 영향을 미쳐왔다.

2 다른 경우 자연재해는 과거뿐 아니라 오늘날에도 오랜 시간과 넓은 지역에 엄청난 영향력을 미친다.

3 고대인류학의 이론에 따르면, 10만년 전 동아프리카 지역의 대가뭄이 인간의 진화사를 크게 바꾸어 놓았다고 한다.

4 현대유전학에서는, 현존하는 인류의 조상은 이때의 자연재해를 견뎌낸 약 2천명의 사람들로 추정한다.

5 이들 섬은 매우 다양한 인류문화와 생물학적 종의 본거지다.

Chapter 10

Translation and its Genres

What to Translate?

Translation is divided into two genres: literary and non-literary. This division implies that literary translation has a longer history than the other and that literary translation has enjoyed more attention than the non-literary. The Korean word for translator is *bunyokka*, meaning '*artist* of translating', which also gives hint at what kind of text Korean translators began to work on. Now the more common way of calling such a profession is *bunyoksa*, meaning '*specialist* in translating.' In the translation classroom, non-literary translation is mainstream while in translation studies, literary translation still seems to attract much academic attention. The closest subgenre to the literary translation in the non-literary translation is subtitling. Similar to the job of a poet, subtitlers have to carefully choose the wording of their adaptations.

Non-literary translation now has its own name: practical translation. Thus, from the standpoint of the practical translation, the literary translation seems impractical. A typical literary translation is the translation of poems, novels and plays. As you may notice, literary translation is mostly done by poets, novelists, and playwrights. To put it succinctly, all translations, except translations of literary works, are practical translations. But in many cases it is very difficult to draw a line between the two genres of translation. Some technical, or very practical, text has literary elements in it, and vice versa. Subtitlers often find themselves straddling both practical and literary territory.

Another division in translation is *print translation* and *film translation,* depending on whether translations appear on paper or on screen. As we now are living in the time of paperless (or less-paper) offices, we read text more often on screen than on paper. That's the reason why we call film translation screen translation. Screen translation is a broader concept including film translation as one of its subgenres. Screen translators are under tighter space and time constraints than print translators, or translators in proper.

Text for Translation

1 자연환경을 보호하는 것이 사람에게도 이롭다는 것은 이제 다 아는 사실이지만, 자연은 아직도 몸살을 앓고 있다.

⇨ While many people have **come to believe** that preserving substantial parts of the natural environment is good for us, Nature is still very much **under attack.**

One big problem has been that natural areas are typically given little economic value.

2 과거, 기획이나 개발 당국은 자연 그대로는 어떤 유용함도 줄 수 없다
고 생각하여 자연에 인위적인 변경을 가했다.

⇨ In past times, planners and developers had **little choice but to alter**
such natural areas, since they appeared to contribute no useful
product or service.

In contrast, their value as land for development was both understandable
and easily calculated. Recently, new ways to calculate the value of natural
areas before development have shown that they provide critical services
of significant financial value. Now we can see more clearly that Nature
pays its own way.

Here, when we speak of Nature, we mean the activities of all the
interactive ecological units on our planet. These ecological units depend
upon physical resources, climatic conditions and all the life forms that
interact there. Global ecology is enabled by large- scale processes that
unify the different regions of the world. These processes have resulted
from more than 4 billion years of chemical, geological, and biological
interaction on planet Earth. When we destroy or degrade soils, oceans,
coasts, wetlands, rivers, lakes, forests, or grasslands, we hurt ourselves by
diminishing the free and important environmental services they provide.
Let's discuss this further.

3 자연이 공짜로 우리에게 주는 경제적 서비스 중 하나는 물을 이용한

수송, 즉 수운이다.

⇨ **One of the most important** commercial services provided free by Nature is transportation by water.

Shipping is by far the most economic method of moving large amounts of goods. For this, we need not be concerned about quality of water, only quantity. Even so, policies affecting water supply can sometimes affect shipping. For example, agricultural practices that promote desertification can dry up water courses and require a more expensive movement of goods over land or by air. This happened to the Aral Sea.

Even more important for mankind, is the vast amount of wild resources provided by Nature. From tropical forests, in particular, many kinds of nuts and fruits are gathered from wild plants. From oceans, lakes, rivers and wetlands are harvested many species of marine mammals, birds, fishes, crustaceans, mollusks, and seaweed for food and other uses. Birds and mammals are hunted in many other areas as well. Best of all, when these resources are taken with intelligent restraint, and the critical role of biodiversity is supported, Nature can sustain such harvesting indefinitely.

A good way to think about biodiversity is that optimum productivity of a habitat is best supported by the interaction of certain numbers of organisms, belonging to a certain mix of species. This condition is supported by Nature's role as a genetic reservoir.

Natural ecosystems also retain many minor species that may have valuable abilities that become important from time to time. These reservoirs are also available when a region is sterilized by natural disasters such as volcanic activity, and need to be re-colonized by living things.

4 이런 이유로, 인간이 자연에 지나치게 간섭하지 않더라도, 자연은 최적의 종의 다양성을 알아서 스스로 유지한다.

⇨ For these reasons, if we do not interfere too much, Nature **tends to** establish and maintain optimum biodiversity all by itself.

This is good for us.

Another hugely important group of natural services supports human agriculture. This starts with soil: a mix of organic matter and rock particles of various sizes (pebbles, sand, clay). Highly productive soil is a dynamic ecosystem in which small living animals mingle with stone particles, bacteria, fungi, air, and water. Generation of good soil can take hundreds to tens of thousands of years. For this reason, rich soils have long been recognized as national treasure, even though massive erosion of this 'black gold' occurs during farming in many countries.

5 야생식물이 토양을 덮으면 뿌리는 토양을 잡아주고, 잎사귀는 빗방울에 의한 토양 침식을 막아준다.

⇨ Where soil is covered by wild plants, their roots hold the soil together, and the leaf cover **stops falling raindrops from** eroding the soil surface. Healthy soil provides at least three services important for agriculture. First, it provides a granular matrix that supports the roots and lower stems of plants. Second, the organic matter in the soil soaks up water; then slowly releases it, giving plants and fungi more time to use the water well. Having more water in the soil also assists in the third service. Because it is rich in numbers of bacteria and fungi, soil is an excellent recycler of organic matter. Dead leaves and animal parts are quickly **decomposed**^{분해} into nutrients. The water dissolves these nutrients and distributes them so that they can be recovered and used to grow new plant, fungal and microbial biomass. When massive amounts of artificial fertilizers and pesticides are used to increase crop yields, natural soils are sterilized and can no longer function as they once did. After this, the necessary nutrients must all be bought and applied^{뿌리다} on the land by the farmers. Because this is expensive, little is applied and food grown under these conditions is not very nutritious.

Nature also supports agriculture with natural pollination.^{가루받이} Most plants require genetic material from other plants to produce healthy fruit or other seed products. Wind and rain may move pollen around and get the job done in some cases. In other cases; however, plants and animals have evolved into specific partnerships. Many plants with flowers produce pollen that is spread by particular animals. These are most commonly species of bats, bees, flies, or hummingbirds. If natural pollinators are destroyed by pesticides, for example, crops will fail unless pollinated by hand. The result is that the volume of crops produced this way is smaller, and the produce more expensive.

Naturally existing animals provide one additional service that supports agriculture – pest^{해충} control.

6 추정치에 따르면, 해충의 99%가 천적, 숙주, 그리고 병원균에 의해 통제된다.

⇨ **Estimates are that** as many as 99% of the potential pests of crops are restrained by a combination of natural predators, parasites and
병원균
pathogens.

For example, gardens with many small birds, certain wasps, spiders, and ladybugs will have a lot less produce damaged by pests, than will gardens without them. When pesticides are used, the small predators are also killed off. After the first season, pesticide resistant insects and other pests have grown **in numbers** and **before long**, cannot be controlled very well.

At the root of all natural productivity is the transformation of energy into biomass. This is done in two ways. One way, chemical energy in
열수
dark places – like caves and ocean-hydrothermal vents – may be transformed into biomass by bacteria. These become the food for several kinds of dark ecosystems. Another way and more importantly, solar energy is transformed into the biomass of surface plants and algae. This biomass, directly or indirectly, feeds all the other living things on the entire planet. Without this large-scale transformation of solar energy into biomass at no cost, we could not live as we do. Many of us would not live at all.

On a much larger scale, Nature stabilizes our global climate and moderates temperature extremes. In modern times, the amounts of the gasses in our atmosphere are strongly influenced by biological activities. Nitrogen, oxygen, carbon dioxide, and methane are the most important gasses recycled by natural processes. By controlling carbon dioxide, in particular, greenhouse heating is moderated by Nature.

7 동시에 물은 다양한 형태로 변신하면서 뜨거운 적도지역에서 다른 지역으로 열을 분산시키는 역할을 수행한다.

⇨ At the same time, the presence of water in all its forms, **serves to** transfer heat from the hottest equatorial regions to cooler regions.

Together, these two processes allow Nature to keep Earth at a livable temperature. By comparison, the temperature at the surface of our moon, with no Life, atmosphere, or water, ranges from 100℃ in the light, to -150℃ in the dark.

Finally, let's consider how Nature sometimes transfers resources from one storage region to another. In the first example, the resource is water. All vascular plants move water through their roots from the soil, up their stems and into their leaves. From there, the water evaporates out of the leaf pores and enters the air as water vapor. Where there are a lot of plants, as in forests or grasslands, quite large amounts of water are extracted from the soil and released into the air. In some cases, this can be sufficient to alter local rainfall patterns. In all cases, the humidity in and near large surface masses of plants, is much higher than over bare soil.

In our second example, the resources transferred are nutrients. Consider the fish known as salmon. Salmon eggs hatch in cold streams or rivers as tiny fish. Then the tiny fish make their way downstream to the ocean. There, most of them end up as food for predators. In the best cases, large numbers of adult salmon return to the streams of their birth, where they mate, lay eggs; then die. With their death, they pass on all the nutrients gathered during their several years in the ocean, to the local habitat where their young will start their lives. At the same time, the initial presence of large numbers of fish, and their later enrichment of the area, also benefits all the other animals and people in the area.

These and many other environmental services are currently provided by Nature at no cost to people. The processes by which they are provided are complicated. Nature has no anger or need for revenge, as some seem to believe, but its activities can be interfered with.

8 이런 과정을 이해하고 자연과 동참할 여유를 우리 인간이 가질 수만 있다면, 자연은 앞으로도 계속 인간에게 봉사할 것이다.
⇨ **Only if** we take the time to understand these processes, and work with Nature, can we expect these critical services to continue as they are.

At present, mankind has the technology to provide many of these services, but not cheaply, and certainly not on a global scale.

9 자연의 경제적 가치를 알 수 있는 좋은 방법은 자연과 똑같은 기능을 인간의 기술로 대체할 때 드는 비용을 계산해 보면 된다.
⇨ Now we can see that a very good way to judge the economic value of natural areas is to estimate **what it would cost to get** the same services using human technology.

When this is done, it immediately becomes clear that careful conservation of these critical environmental services is the best economic policy for mankind, if we want to continue to live as we do now.

1 under attack

2 no[little] choice but to do something

3 one of the most + adjective + nouns

4 tend to do something

5 stop something from doing something

6 Estimates are that S + V

7 in numbers

8 before long

9 serve to do something

10 only if S + V

Model Dialogue

Amy: Nature is under attack by humans.

James: Humans have no choice but to develop natural environments so that they can squeeze the most out of the land and seas. Sometimes people have to destroy one of the most scenic views to reserve more water and generate more power.

Amy: But we have to stop people from destroying Mother Nature more. Nature serves us better by itself without being interfered with by humans.

James: Only if there are enough resources to support people. But that's only a dream.

Amy: You know what? Trees in the Amazon Basin are being cut down in astonishing numbers. Before long we'll have to buy canned air just like we buy bottled water now.

James: Don't worry. Estimates are that trees worldwide could support humans for another 100 years. By the way, why don't you think that people are sometimes under attack from Nature?

Talking Practice

Now, the class divides into two groups. The two groups of students sit in line facing each other. Each pair of students will talk about the topic using the expressions for 5 minutes. After each talking session is finished, students will move anticlockwise to talk to a new partner for another 5 minutes. Talking Practice ends when students meet their first partner again.

▶ Following is part of the main text. Fill the blanks to complete the text (1 point for each blank).

The New Urban Design movement holds strong views on streets. First, 1_____ should not divide communities or endanger children. Within neighborhoods, traffic speeds should be slow, roads narrow, and pedestrians should have free 2_____ to the streets. Such streets should join communities, not separate them, because this would reduce the efficiency of emergency services, mass transit, and deliveries. Streets should have a lot of plant and tree _3___ to provide beauty and shade. There should also be arrangements for water to drain into the soil beside the streets, rather than running directly into sewers or flooding the area. In urban business areas, 4_____ should be along streets and should not be plentiful. The goal is to have people utilize 5_____, rather than their cars, when they move into the urban center. Since this can challenge certain businesses, a good mass transit system must be in place and widely available to the downtown area.

▶ Translate into English as they appear in the main text. (3 points each)

1 일정 공간에 사는 사람의 숫자가 많아질수록, 돈벌이의 기회도 많아진다.

2 가능하면, 현지에서 생산되어야 한다.

3 이런 경관을 일반인들이 이용하게끔 하는 것은 지역사회에 매우 긍정적인 영향을 준다.

4 이러한 지침은 상가와 주택지역을 적절히 혼합하는 것을 매우 중요하게 다룬다.

5 과거에 비해 오늘날의 도시계획은 인간복지를 매우 중요시하는 추세다.